The Diaries of a T Bouncers and

By STU ARMSTRONG

ISBN-13: 978-1497589322   ISBN-10: 1497589320

"Last night when I finished my shift all I wanted to do

was go home and sleep, but on the way I chased and

caught a man that had stolen a woman's handbag and

reunited her with it, she was so drunk she didn't know

where she was, I made sure that she was safe and put her

into a taxi to get her home. Just as I was near to my car I

saw three lads beating the living shit out of one lad, I

chased them off and checked he was

ok............................ I bet you don't see that on

YouTube!"

"Sometimes in life, the only thing that you can do to

combat violence is to use a greater proportion of violence,

with some people it's all that they understand"

Best Wishes
Stu

Dedication

This, my second book, is dedicated to the most important people in my life, quite simply to Ben, Luca and Sol.

You inspire me to be a better person, you give me a reason for life, you are the reason that my heart beats.

I strive every day of my life to be the very best Dad that I can be, I know I am not the best but no father could ever love their children more than I love mine.

For you Boys, I love You!

Always Dad x

Acknowledgments

Again I have to say a big thank you to Robin Barratt www.robinbarratt.com and Steve Wraith www.playersincevents.co.uk for the inspiration to achieve a lifelong ambition of writing a book.

Thank you to my good friend Scott Telfer, for his fantastic work producing the cover once again, to Hayden Parker for his help at all hours of the day and night and to my Mother, Celia Armstrong for proof reading. Without you all this book could never have been produced.

I suppose that I really should also say thanks to the legions of complete Pissheads, Knobheads, Drunken Retards and Totally out and Out Fuckups that have kept me in a job for all of these years. I would also like to say a big thank you for all of the help and support that I have had from the members of my online forum 'UK Bouncers'.

Top bunch of people & top banter, long may it stay the biggest & best group of its kind.
www.facebook.com/groups/ukbouncers
One last note to all of you Bouncers, Doorman, Door Supervisors or whatever the fuck you want to call yourself out there.
"Have a safe one and make it home in one piece!"

Contents

A Word from the Author

I hope that you enjoy my book. This is my second book, and it's been written by popular demand and amazing feedback and I would like to make it clear again from the outset that I have not written this book to claim that I am the world's best Doorman, to play the big 'I am'. I have also not written this book to play the hard man, like many other Bouncers have done in the past with their's.

To the piss takers out there, and I am sure there will be many. I just want to say, I don't care what you think, I wanted to write a book and become published and I have, and loads of people bought it, and I got great reviews and I have written another one so HA bollocks to you!!

Being a Doorman is a job, nothing more, nothing less, sometimes good, very often not so good. I do the job, but I don't live the so called Bouncers life style, which to be honest I think has pretty much died off. It's just a job like any other.

Yeah sure, it can be dangerous and yes, you can get hurt, which I have been on more than one occasion. But you can also get bored, cold, tired and sometimes totally fed up, and it also screws up relationships and impedes on family time and that is the worst thing in the world.

So just remember next time you have a night out that the Bouncers are no different to you. They are doing their job, most likely for their families, just the same as you. So say hello, show some respect and I guarantee that you will get the same back. My way, right or wrong is to treat people with respect. Show some respect and nine times out of ten you will be given respect back.

Just think for a moment, would you like to do our job? Could you do our job? Standing around in the cold, rain, sleet and snow, yet still opening the door for you. Greeting you with a smile. Still poised ready to see who wants to take a crack at you tonight.

The quietest nights are the worst, the most boring and the most tiring. Standing there for hours with your brain and body ready to react within a fraction of a second, to god only knows what.

So could you do it? Would you do it? Remember if it wasn't for the excellent Door staff in this country, then bars, clubs and anywhere else that sell alcohol would be nothing but anarchy!

We make pubs, clubs, nightclubs and all other kinds of venues safe for you to enjoy. So next time you see some horror video of a Bouncer online just ask yourself, is this the whole story that I can see? Did something happen beforehand? Just what was the catalyst? It's human nature just to go for the action shots but they don't give you the full picture of the incident. So next time you see something like this then please give that a thought.

Yeah, I can be a complete bastard I suppose, if I have to be, but I am only a bastard to bastards. Show me respect I will give the same back, don't and I won't. Simple. So for whatever reason you are asked to leave a venue then just leave the venue, you don't need the grief and sure as hell the doorman doesn't either!

No doubt he has had grief all night and will get even more later on. I have written this book because all of my life I have had a love of books, of reading and of the written world. So here it is. Good, bad or ugly this is my book. Hope that you enjoy it!

Stu Armstrong

CHAPTER ONE

The Singing Doorman

Well you will have heard of the singing Policeman but have you ever heard of the singing Doorman? Well that was me about 13 years ago now over in Swallwell in Gateshead.

A so called mate of mine at the time known as 'Squeaky' because of him camp voice and his wife had just got a pub over the river in Swallwell at the bottom of Whickham Bank called 'The Poacher'.

I suppose quite an apt name for Mark 'Squeaky' Gibson, he was, before he got the bar, an, on and off salesman selling fax machines and photocopiers, and just about a full time conman and alcoholic. The amount of people he would sell equipment to and give them a better deal for cash, and then mysteriously the stuff would never arrive was unreal. A real slimy conning robbing bastard this kid was, who used to drink Lager and Vodka, and a lot of it for breakfast.

How the bloody hell he never got done for drink driving I will really never know!

Anyway I was surprised when he announced that he had got a bar, in fact I was shocked who in their right minds would let this kid take over a pub? I think to be fair it was more his wife than him, I felt sorry for her she was a grafter not a thief like Squeaky, and the amount of shit she had to put up with because of him just wasn't on, not long later there was a celebration when they got divorced!

It was a decent size bar with a large conservatory set on the back where they would serve food, a smaller back bar and a large bar at the front. When they first took over they had bits of bother but nothing too bad, but loads of complaints that they no longer had Karaoke on at weekends.

Well in those days I used to be out a lot and was bit of a Karaoke freak, in fact I used to cover for a mate and run the Karaoke some times in the Alnwick Castle in North Shields.

The Alnwick was my Dad's old bar but was at the time being run by an old bloke called Eddy, a notoriously dodgy little old fucker that would have your eyes out and come back for the sockets if he could and who was colloquially known to the regulars as 'Frog Eyes' due to his sunken in yet, popping out eyes that did actually make him resemble a frog.

When 'Frog Eyes' first took over true to form he was quite difficult to get any money out of, if you were owed it, and my mate Pip jacked the Karaoke in.

Well old 'Frog Eyes' brought in his own Karaoke gear in and tried to run it himself, which was fucking painful due to the fact that he couldn't sing for toffee, in fact he thought he sung like Sinatra but he sounded like a couple of screaming cats fighting in a back lane in the middle of the night, but he really truly believed that he was the boyo. In fact if there was an over 70's category in the X-Factor then this fucker would have been on it!

So somehow along the line me and one of my oldest mates from back in Junior School and who I am still mates with to this day, Scott, took over running it, mainly just for a laugh and for beer.

Anyway 'Squeaky Gibson used to drink in there then and loved the old 'Hokey Cokey Karaoke' and the way that we did it, to be fair mind we were fucking good! Had everyone having a cracking laugh, which if you ask me that's what it's all about!

The way that we ran these Karaoke shows was for a laugh, if you got someone up to sing who strutted up and thought they were fucking Elvis and some kind of local star just because they could sing a little bit were made to sound like a bag of saggy old shite, a few twists of the knobs and presses on the button of the mixer and job done, but on the other hand when people were crap but just wanted to do it for a laugh then we tried our very best to work some magic and make them sound better.

Anyway that soon went south when Eddy upset all the locals and didn't pay his bills, so me and Scott along with Tony my other mate, who also happened to be Eddies Son, more of less took over the bar for the last couple of weeks before it was closed down and ran it like our own private nightclub.

Opening on the Friday morning we didn't close and ran straight through all day and all night losing all track of time taking advantage of not paying for any beer and drinking all night, before we knew it was Saturday morning then Sunday, then Monday, this happened again all week and through the following weekend until the Monday morning when the Police closed down the pub. We had made a killing being open nonstop and not locking the doors once in a full ten days.

Well 'Frog Eyes' had promised to pay us but he didn't bother his arse, surprise surprise but that wasn't too bad as we just kept the takings and split it between us, which to be honest, wasn't that much as we had been drinking for free *for ten days solid as had all of our mates and a good few birds that we had pulled in Whitley Bay and took down there for a drinking binge and then a lot more, but that's another story* ☺

The Alnwick Castle – North Shields

So the pub was closed down but we still had shit loads of stock left so we made a deal with the bloke who had a pub just round the corner the Maggy Bank, the bloke that owned it, who always wanted to appear above reproach but deep down was as slippery as they come, so him and his 'Fugly' daughter affectionately known in the area as 'The Pig in the Wig', had the cellar doors open about 6am one morning and me and Tony loaded bottle after bottle of alcohol into my 'Four Wheel Drive' and delivered it for a nice wedge of cash, which we split with Scott.

Early on the Sunday morning me and Tony had went into the bar and filled the huge bottle bins, normally filled with empties with full bottles and managed to heave them onto the back of my Jeep, we had a few runs and finally got all the gear shifted.

We managed to sell the lot to him more or less, he took everything apart from the kegs, so undeterred we sold the kegs to another local bar just next to the Tyne Tunnel called the Duke of Wellington, oh and also the payphone which we had ripped off the wall, at the same time as the condom machine's and the sanitary towel machines, which we emptied.

Incidentally it was the 'Pig in the Wig' that put me on Pubwatch in North Shields, for bugger all I may add, I appealed to the committee and was removed from it straight away, Funny fucker she was!

(She had some fetish about getting dressed up in just a PVC Lollypop woman's coat and nothing else – YUK Mind with a face like that she would have been good for road safety as kids wouldn't have dared go near a road, never mind cross it!)

Anyway I digress, this is where I knew Squeaky Gibson from, we got on well at first and he asked me to do a Karaoke and Disco on for him, at his wedding, and to use my big black convertible Jeep as a wedding car, I charged next to nothing but another slippery little shit he tried to rip me off and not pay me, so walking through North Shields Town Centre the week after he got bounced off a Bus Stop and got a slap from a man that may or may have not been me, and hey presto when I got home the cash was through my door.

So when he rang me and asked me to do Karaoke for him three nights a week in Swallwell, Friday, Saturday and Sunday at first I said no, but at the time I had just been made redundant from my day job and was working part time doing the books for a local printing factory, I also by now had a baby on the way, my Ben and money was tight, so I thought what the hell and said I would do it on the promise of payment in cash each night and free beer.

So the first week I get there having never been in the bar before it seemed not to bad, it had a couple of doorman on, a couple of proper big lumps who had worked there for a good while, couple of canny lads but they didn't look happy.

When I had a bit crack with them it turned out that Squeaky had not paid them for the two weeks that he had been there, they told me that on Sunday night when they finished if they weren't paid then they were going to take the till, "I don't fucking blame you I told them", and come Sunday did they get paid? Did they shite, so the next thing the two Bouncers were over the bar one of them taking Squeaky down with a cracking right hook on the way, basically took the till and the contents and I can't say I blamed them!

I wished to god I had a video camera with me, it was funny as fuck, this was well before the days of smart phones and camera phones and Facebook but it would have gone viral, in fact I am chuckling away to myself right now writing this.

So next week, you guessed it no Bouncers and I don't blame them so over to fucking muggings here, luckily you didn't get that much bother which is just as well as I soon found myself running the Karaoke and ragging people out at the same time, as soon as I saw something from the corner of the bar I would whack the longest song on I had, hurdle the DJ booth and multitasked as a Bouncer. In fact after a while I soon became famous for switching people's requests to the Don McLean lengthy classic 'American Pie', a classic maybe but a stupidly long song but it suited my needs perfectly.

The Poacher – Swallwell (Later renamed the Gamekeeper)

I soon got used to this and it wasn't a bad bar to be honest, I even arranged a stag night there for my mate and on Sunday Night's used to often take Dave my father in law at the time over with me and buy him a few beers. He came over for the lads stag night and it was a funny old night, I had booked him a Rolly Polly Gram, and had arranged to meet her outside the bar at 9pm, so as I sneaked out followed by a couple of lads to wait for her to turn up and was taking the piss out of the lads saying to them 'I bet your lass or one of your ex's turns up.

Then up pulled a car and out of the back she came, and if you had seen my face when I heard her shouting "Stu, Stu I didn't know it was you!" well the two lads just pissed themselves laughing as Sue comes over to me hugging me and kissing me. Sue, bit of legend in North Shields and regular at the time in the Alnwick, I had known her for years, a big hearted very kind women that never seemed to speak ill of anyone, and the same to this day. (She later went on to be in the program Geordie Shore on one episode, with the complete bell ends who seem to think there typical Geordies – Bunch of complete fucking wankers)

Anyway it was a cracking night and there were a few people there from where I had previously worked in a day job, Sage where I was a Network Support Technician, anyway when we were locking up and everyone had gone me and Dave were sitting having a pint and the mortal mess that was my mate at the time Harry Mann was knocking at the door with two lads who I didn't know but were at the stag night.

I opened up and he said I just want to see you for minute mate, drunk out of his skull he staggers in and starts saying he had a great night and starts hugging me, and then out on nowhere the little bastard bites me on the side of my neck drawing blood, so quick as a flash me being sober as well I dropped him, booooom crack straight to his jaw which just felled him where he stood.

Unfortunate, I thought for me at the time, as it was for him when he went down I heard CRACCCCKKK, that was the sound of his head smashing off the side of the stone fireplace, you could hear the silence then as I think everyone in the room were thinking the same as me, he is going in a coffin and I was going to jail! But thank goodness he came round after about a minute and didn't have any lasting damage, as soon as he came round I stood him up and slung him out, where his two big daft mates were standing, who started all verbal and on and on they went, and to be honest they were never going to do anything, you know the kind 'all the gear but no idea', anyway after a listening to their slaver for a few minutes I turned round and said "Look lads, your boring me now, do yourselves a favor and off you fuck". And they did which made me laugh as I shut the doors.

A few weeks after this Squeaky Gibson turned up at my front door and said that he had split up with his Mrs. and wasn't in the pub any longer, he blamed her but I was skeptical and when I went to work on the Friday and spoke to his Mrs. she told me that he had been having it away with some real skank from the bar, and hadn't paid a single bill since they went into the bar. The non-payment of bills, well that didn't surprise me one little bit but screwing this skank did surprise me as he was always pissed, I later found out that he was an alcoholic, and didn't seem to have the energy to pull a pint never mind shag some skank.

Anyway I carried on working there for a while but my nights were cut and it was time for a change to be honest, I liked working the door properly not this Karaoke/Doorman shite so I started to look around for a new place, when I think about what happened next in hindsight I must have been stupid, but hey these things happen.

Guess who I went to work for next? Yep you guessed it Squeaky Gibson the Alcoholic who didn't pay his bills, god only knows how but he managed to get a bar himself, the Wagon Way at forest Hall. My old stomping ground from when I used to be the Manager of the Musketeer years before. The only problem was it was the same deal, Karaoke / Door, I wasn't too keen but needed a change and, well to be honest it was the easiest work that I have ever done.

The Wagon was a fucking rough bar but the locals sort of kept themselves in check so I didn't once have to chuck anyone out. On my first night up there I was surprised when I walked in to see who was standing behind the bar, a bloke known in North Shields as 'Dangerous Brian', I had known him for a few years and had even worked a door with him once. I asked him why he was there and he said that he was helping Squeaky get set up, I thought no more off it at the time, he was an ok kind of bloke at times but a real Walter Mitty type character who had been there and done it all, or so he said, another one of these ex Royal Marines. Yeah Right!

It turned out sometime later that Squeaky didn't want him there but he just moved in and refused to leave, haha what a complete cowardly little bastard Squeaky was. As time moved on Squeaky started seeing, my wife at the times mate, a lass called Sam, well they suited each other down to the ground.

I have never in my life met anyone with as many issues as Sam, this lass was seriously fucked in the head. Every time she had a drink she would kick off and start to cry about the brother that had died in a car accident about ten or more years previous.

A funny looking lass, a little fat dwarfy looking ugly cunt of a thing with hair like a Gollywog, a real little 'Fugly' little 'Munter' who had been engaged to some bloke a few years before and they had bought a house together. Well anyway he must have went to Specsavers one day and realized just what an ugly little 'Umpa Lumpa' he had saddled himself with and he started shagging his ex, and only went and got her pregnant and fucked Sam off hahaha I wish I had seen that!

Well maybe because of this or maybe because she knew what she looked like she was just so desperate for a man, any man, would do, in fact most of my mates had mercy fucked her when they were comptley rat-arsed. Ha they all regretted it and never did it more than once!!!

So you guessed it she ended up with squeaky, who was also shagging a slag from behind the bar and some Skank that used to turn up every now and again. Well after about three weeks, and don't forget he was still married he only went and proposed to her, she accepted and off he went to Argos for the cheapest fake engagement ring that he could find.

The week after I had a night off and me and Nicki my wife and Squeaky and Sam the 'Umpa Lump' went for a drink to celebrate and ended up back at the Wagon after time, the four of us were sitting having a drink and Dangerous Brian was fannying about behind the bar and I think to be honest he felt left out as all of a sudden out of nowhere I heard SMASHHHH and a pint glass that he had just thrown smashed very close to Nicki, well his face said it all as I jumped up and ran at him behind the bar.

Anyway Dangerous Brian had Epilepsy and was prone to having fits or faking fits, or both we were never quite sure, It wouldn't have been so bad if it had nearly hit me but I kicked off big time as it nearly hit Nicki as he ran through the hatch out of the other side of the bar I was shouting come on then see how you like it you fucking wanker, and started pelting Pint glasses at him, and his reaction? Yup you guessed it he had a fit. Rolling round on the floor frothing at the mouth I was pretty sure that he was putting it on but wasn't sure, I remember thinking I should dump him in the bath with some washing powder and some washing to save using the washer.

I had a feeling he was faking but still not sure, so I did what all good first aid trained people would to in this situation, kicked the cunt into the corner of the bar and left him there, fake or fit I didn't really give a fuck after what he had just done!

Well the next Friday night when I got there the pub was surrounded by Police and all of the punters were coming out of the fire exits, strange I thought so I went in and the bar was full of coppers. By all accounts Dangerous Brian was mortal and had been playing pool with two locals that were a bit handy, some argument started and Brian started playing the big man and smashed one of them in the face, so they both basically smashed seven kinds of shit out of him with Pool cues, and knocked him out, and guess what happened? When he came round he rang the Police and then had a fit.

I couldn't help but laugh as somebody had stuffed a beer mat in his gob and shoved him in the corner and just left him, so when I walked in and found out what had happened, Squeaky told me and I said "Where's Dangerous Brian then?", "Over there he says" and points in the corner and there he was lying there on his back with foam round his mouth and a beer mat between his teeth unconscious (Yeah Right)!

Well that was the beginning of the end, the Police were checking up on the bar and it turned out that Squeaky didn't have a license to open the pub, not just that night it turned out that he has never ever had a license, in fact he hadn't even applied for one! What a complete Mug.

So the Police shut the pub down, and quick as a flash I picked up his bunch of keys that he would always leave lying around and ran to the safe. Took a few hundred quid out for wages that I wouldn't get from this week and the week after and even left him an IOU note. Shut the safe chucked the keys at him and fucked off for a pint.

He was booted out of the pub next day by the bailiff's and the pub never ever opened again, it has since been knocked down. So remember if you have a decent pub that you want totally fucked then Squeaky is your man! If you can find him, he just vanished after that!

Oh, and the little fat Umpa Lumpa, what happened to her I hear you ask? Well she found out about the 'Skanks' he was slipping it to and dumped him, but that only lasted a day, they got back together and then, when he just vanished she just cried and winged on for weeks. No fucking change there then, and went on to be so desperate for a bloke that she would let anyone who had enough drink and / or d rugs inside them to fuck her. Trust me I don't know anyone who would do this horrible fucker sober!

And Dangerous Brian? Well he seemed to disappear out of the area for a while, and then turned up again for a while and then who knows? Personally I couldn't give a fuck. I never ever forgave him for the Pint Glass incident!

CHAPTER TWO

A German, 2 Dutchmen, 5 Pollack's and 7 Irishmen

Funny old night this was, odd to say the least but looking back it was a full moon. Now say what you want but any Doorman worth his salt will tell you that a full moon equals one thing... ... ...DICKHEADS!!

It never fails the amount of bother that you get, its mad, and it's always, always worse on a full moon, there are many theories as to why this is the case but the one that makes sense to me is this:

As everyone knows the Moon has a gravitational force that, in part controls the tides of the sea, along with this is also has an electro magnetically charged field which is stronger and a hell of a lot more prevalent when the moon is full, and as you will know your brain works with a series of electrical signals, well when the electro magnetically charged full moon is out this has an effect on the electrical signals in the brain, very mild but they are there.

Mild that is until you start drinking and then all hell can be let loose in some people turning them violent.

Don't know if this is true or not but it's something that I once heard and it would seem to make sense to me, but if it is or not I don't know but I do know, as do most Bouncers a full moon spells out Dickheads!

Anyway, me and Craig are on the Door at a Bar that we were just covering for one night, a small place with a bit of reputation for trouble, so as we walk up the hill to the isolated Bar that we were working in I look up into the dark winter sky, clear as a bell one of those crisp clear winter nights and there it was, I great big lump of bloody green cheese, better known as a full moon.

"Oh fuck" I say to Craig, "Full Moon, we are in for a fun night!" Craig was pretty new on the Door and hadn't heard of the full moon thing for Doorman as yet, as I explained he started to laugh, "Arr bollocks Stu, so what you're saying the Werewolves will be out tonight?", this made me laugh, "Just wait, you will change your tune by the time we are walking back down the hill mate" I said and then put my head to the sky and started to howl like a Werewolf, "Arrroooooooo Aroooooooooo".

As we approach the bar I remember thinking 'What a fucking shit hole', I opened the door and straight away the smell smacked me in the face, like being hit with 5000 pairs of tramps socks! What a bizarre smell, not so much nasty but fucking terrible! So we see the gaffa and get signed in and sorted out. The Manager says straight off the bat "Go on then get yourselves outside then lads", "Hang about a second mate, I have got some bad news for you" I said, "What's that then" said the gaffa. "Your kettles broken mate" I tell him dead pan serious. Falling right into my hands he says "Nah mate it's not the kettles working fine!" Haha works every time "Really, great stuff thanks I'll have a tea then mate, just bring it out for me" and off we went to the door.

The pub was quite when we started and seemed to get busier as the night went on, after about an hour a group of what looked like contractors came in, about 15 of them. Funny looking group all big blokes apart from one who must have been just under 5ft tall and spoke with a strong Northern Irish accent. In fact looking at him and the accent I reckon he may well have just been a fucking leprecorn!

They seemed ok and all had a bit crack with us on the way in, well it was like the bloody 'United Nations' in the group there was a German, 2 Dutchmen, 5 Pollack's and 7 Irishmen. I never did like Germans as they tried to shoot my Granda in World War Two, when he was a dessert rat. (Didn't fucking get him though did you! Ha) but still not as bad as the French, pack of garlic snail eating cowardly surrender monkeys!

So that night went on and the 'United Nations' were putting the drink away like it was going out of fashion, with every pint they were doing a Jagger Bomb and were well on the way to being completely mashed. All of a sudden I heard breaking glass inside the bar and I ran in and there was one of the Irishmen chucking glasses at a barman, both me and Craig went in I grab the lad chucking the glasses by the arm and say "Right mate come on out, you can't be doing that" and I started to pull him towards the door, changing my grip to a Nelson as he started to struggle, Craig was behind me and then all of sudden he disappeared, as I looked round they all kicked off, apart from the Leprecorn and Craig was trying to push them back, the big German punched me in the back of the head a couple of times and then they started picking up bottles.

What the hell was I going to do now? 15 onto 2, well more like 14.5 thinking about the Leprecorn, I change my hold on the big fella that I had, and I pulled him into a choke hold and shouted at the top of my voice "Get out, go on Fuck off or I will put him to sleep", they all looked and one bloke said "You haven't get the bottle", so as I tightened the pressure around his neck and I could hear him gargling and the telltale sign he was nearly out as his legs seemed to get wobbly, I shouted again "Fuck off now the lot of you", they didn't move so I tightened the grip around his throat with my arm, he was a big strong bloke and I could feel the burning in the muscles in my arm, then down he went, asleep, out cold.

I kept my hold on him and lowered him to the ground while he was still out, as they started closing in on me and Craig, just as this was happening a barman who has got to be the dizziest thickest fucker that I have ever met in my life comes wandering into the middle of it all totally oblivious to what was going on. I gave the sleeping Irishman a kick, just a light one in the ribs and he came round, he didn't know where the hell he was and in a split second I drag him up still in a choke and shout "Get the Fuck out of the bar or he is going to sleep again".

"You'll kill him you mad bastard one of his mates shouted "Yeah and if I let go you will kill us so I may as well take at least one with me, now I mean it fuck off", they called my bluff so again I applied pressure, this time he was down, I still kept him in a hold and this time waited what seemed like hours, but in fact it was only really a few seconds, and he didn't come round so again couple of light kicks in the ribs, that seemed to do it and they started going to the Door, so half for fun, half as I can be a right bastard when the mood takes me I pick this bloke up, run him to the door, open it with his head and then choke him out again as he flew through the door.

They were all milling around outside and sleeping beauty didn't know where the fuck he was at first, and the thick

Barman was standing rooted to the spot shaking with terror. As he realised what was going on and what I had done to him sleeping beauty, who was now across the road with the help of the rest of the United Nations started shouting and issuing the usual threats and then came running at me. I get into a fighting stance and have a fist ready to smash into his temple when he got to me, standing behind me was the manager of the bar, he said in a meek mild voice "Don't Stu mate Don't" the way he said it I knew just what he meant, He wanted me to make an example out of this fucker but wanted to cover his own arse at the same time.

As he came running for me I was preparing to do what I had down many times before, it's a case of using their own weight and velocity against them. Just as they are in front of you and raise the arm to throw the punch you side step and at the same time a straight right to the temple or chin, but what happened next was fucking mint! He was running at me like a man possessed, fist flaying around him like a 'Windmill on Acid', and then he tripped on the curb. Yup, really he tripped on the curb, went down like a bag of old shite and this was him out cold again. Hahaha that was him asleep for the fourth time in just the last few minutes, wanker.

At this his mates picked him up and carried him away, shouting and balling at me on the way, but that's the point. They were on their way.

As I walk back into the bar the dozy barman was still there, and he looked at me mouth open and said "Stu, that was pretty impressive, how did you do that? Did you spray him with something?"

CHAPTER THREE

Manchester Gaz

The story my mate Gaz gave me was that he was on the run in Gran Caneria, from West Ham's notorious ICF (Inter City Firm) who most people back in England had heard of. They would have a been at the peak of their notoriety when led by Cass Pennant. But something didn't ring true about this as he also told me that he had never been out of Manchester in his life until coming over here, but then I thought to myself you just never know, maybe something had happened at a game in Manchester or something like that. Anyway me and Gaz became closer and closer mates, and would often go for something to eat together after work. We happened to stumble on, of all things, an Indian restaurant, but one with a difference.

There was quite a lot of construction work going on, on the island back in the day and a lot of cheap Asian labor was brought across. Well this was a restaurant basically for them. The first time we stumbled across it, half pissed, we went in we got some very funny looks from the owner, staff, and customers being the only white Europeans in there. The meal was amazing and stupidly cheap because it wasn't for holiday makers, or even locals, it catered just really for the Asian migrant workers. On top of the cheapness the authentic Indian food was amazing, none of your bright red Chicken Tikka Masala shit in here.

After ending up there just about every night of the week, both me and Gaz ended up very good friends with the owner Ravi, and his family, and most of the regular punters.

I remember Gaz saying to him, "Any trouble in here, let us know we can sort it out for you" I also remember thinking to myself that Gaz was trying to big us up just a little too much. Ravi's reaction was hilarious and Gaz's face even better. Ravi said "come with me I show you how I deal with trouble, with Lager Louts if they get lost and come here" He took us round behind the small counter come bar area and from underneath pulled a bloody huge knife come machete type thing. The sort of thing that would put Crocodile Dundee right in the shade.

Well Gaz just about shit himself when Ravi took a wild swinging motion with the huge knife as if to chop at Gaz's head, Gaz shouted "No Ravi No!" Ravi and me were both pissing ourselves laughing. Safe to say that Gaz didn't try to big us up with our new mate Ravi anymore. One thing that puzzled me in there was this, a lot of the customers had just come over from India, couldn't speak English, were not really westernized at all and they ate in what I was told was a traditional way in the part of India that they came from which was rural and isolated.

They ate with their hands, scooping up large handfuls of all kinds of wonderful Indian dishes with chapatti's or just with their hands.

One night me and Gaz were persuaded to give it go, both of us a bit worse for the wear we did, and it wasn't too bad at all. But how the fuck did we have stained hands from the curries for the next week? Nothing, and I mean nothing, would get this stuff off, scrubbing with bleach the lot, yet the regulars and their families who ate like this all the time never had so much as a bit of yellow curry stain about them.

Anyway as I said we got know Ravi and his family really well and one day he just stopped charging us all together, he told us that we were his friends and guests.

This really was a top bloke, who all these years later I am still in touch with, he now lives on the UK not far from Leeds and my god has he come a long way? He has a string of restaurants and even diversified into importing as a wholesaler in bulk Indian cooking ingredients.

I went down to see he him a few years back and his restaurant couldn't be any different from the one in Gran Caneria back in the day, a beautiful, amazing place, with amazing prices to match, bloody expensive amazing prices, but still he wouldn't charge me. Top bloke! It turns out he still has the place in Gran Caneria but the crappy area off to the side of the town was taken over by tourism some years before and its changed a lot. I couldn't believe it when he showed me the photos, one thing Ravi is good at is making money it would seem. He will sell you a quality meal in pleasant surroundings with great service, but fuck me he will have your eyes out when the bill comes for the privilege. Well good luck to him I say.

The more that I got to know Gaz the better we got on and he eventually moved over from his bar to mine and I have got to say we made a bloody good team, it wasn't like working a door in England in a lot of respects, I would say that back then the drunken behavior was worse, the violence was worse and very often we had a huge communication problem with a lot of Spaniards and god forbid if you gave one of the Spaniards a slap as by the end if the night the whole sodding family would be waiting outside for you, often including the mother and even the grandmother it really was a fucking family affair! As I was later to find out the hard way!

Anyway me and Gaz ended up really good mates but there was always something that didn't ring true, it was obvious that he was running away from something or someone but his tale of the ICF just didn't ring true to me. He never talked about home, or his mates or his family.

So this day I am driving along the road after just staggering out of bed and I see Gaz walking along with two lads that I have never seen before, I toot and wave in a hurry and he waves back, that night at work he told me that these two were his two best mates from Manchester and they were over to see him for a few days. They turned up at the bar later on and were blatantly fucked of their skulls and one of them just reminded me of Shaun Ryder from the Happy Mondays. They seemed like good lads but off their Tits.

When we locked up Gaz asked me if he could take the next night of work to hit the bars with his mates, I agree and get a lad in to cover and he invites me to meet them in a local nightclub after work, I thought why the hell not! Dirty Women and Dirty Beer! What's not to like???

Little did I know where I would actually be after work, it wasn't going to be a fucking nightclub!

Is was a busy night at work as a couple of flights had landed, we chucked out a load of lads for generally being dickheads, and not for the first time a local prostitute who was trying to ply her trade in the bar. Dirty old skank that she was, she must have been in her mid-forties, and had a face like she had been hit with the ugly stick more than once

and that yellow jaundice looking tinge to her skin that made it obvious that she was a smackhead. She had a Sunderland

accent and was known locally as the 'Minging Makum'. She had managed to sneak in while we were scuffling with the group of lads that we had chucked out earlier. As was standard she didn't want to leave and started winging on and then her catch phrase "Let me stay man, go on, let me stay I will suck your cock, and your mates" to which came my standard reply which I thought was rather polite, "Off you fuck you skank, they don't call the Minging Makem for nothing!"

So near the end of the night I hear a bit of a commotion and there Gaz and he mates, mortal and off his lips, but Gaz for whatever reason was bollock naked! They started coming towards my bar and Gaz stopped them and said "Nah, Stu's my mate and I work there, respect for my mate we are not even trying to get in". Off they went with Gaz shouting "Stu, see you in a bit mate!"

So I finished work, got locked up with the help of Stevie the stand-in Bouncer and had a couple of cheeky liveners in the form of some of Russia's finest and off I went to meet Gaz and the lads. Stevie was invited but didn't want to come. As I get to the nightclub I go and talk to the lads on the door and they say "Stu, we have done it for you not for that prick Gaz", confused at what Billy the head doorman was saying I said "Eh? Done what, Oh fuck what's he done?", they pointed to a dark alley up the side of the club and said we put him up there, we dumped him there but took his two mates on the beach and kicked the fuck out of them, but we didn't do Gaz in out of respect for you, but you better tell the cunt, he don't come back in here again, ever, cos next time he will go on the beach and I will drown the cunt!"

Billy didn't elaborate any more so I went up the ally and was shocked at what I found but suddenly it all made sense, the someone or something that Gaz was hiding from, I straight away knew what it was. There he was slumped on the ground unconscious and lying next to him was a syringe. Dirty fucking smackhead! I found out later that the three of them had been caught shooting up in Billy's club. Heroin that's what Gaz was hiding from, and looks like his mates had brought his nemesis with them.

At first I thought he was dead, I couldn't find a pulse or any sign of breathing, then a very faint pulse. I ran back to the door of the club and shouted "Billy, Billy mate I am sorry, he deserves a good fucking kicking, do me one more favor and help me carry him to a taxi mate". He did and all credit to him as Gaz had fucked up, and fucked up grandly in Billy's club. We struggled to get him into the back of the taxi, he was a big lump and out of it. I got the taxi driver to take us to the hospital and it seemed to take forever, about half way there Gaz came round, I sat him up and lifted his head and what happened next will never leave me.

He looked at me directly into my eyes and very slowly and very quietly like it was the most difficult thing in the world to say the few little words that were barely audible. "Stu, thank you for being a friend, I tried to get away but it followed me and now it's got me", "Gaz for fucks sake why didn't you tell me" I said, then he managed to get out what would be his very last words "I was ashamed, I am ashamed this thing owns me". With that he slumped backwards and I just knew. Manchester Gaz was gone.

So in the back of a taxi on a holiday island off the coast of North Africa came the end of Manchester Gaz, he died in my arms.

Heroin is a terrible drug, it takes not only your body but your mind and it always kills you in end, it takes you into a different world, the kind of world that there is only one thing that you care about, and that's getting more brown for your next hit, and it doesn't matter what you have to do to get it.

R.I.P. Manchester Gaz.

At least you're away from it all now.

CHAPTER FOUR

Derby Day

All over the UK when it comes to football nothing seems to beat a local derby, but none so much as the famous, and sometimes infamous, Tyne and Wear derby between Newcastle United and Sunderland.

Geordies against Makum's, Tyne against Wear it's a bloody big thing up here, I can't see why myself but there you go, as far as I am concerned football is just a game played by overpaid 'Nancy Boys' and I really can't be arsed with it.

Leading up to this particular derby game I think a lot of people were a little wary, for want of a better word. The last derby game between these two teams was played at St James Park in Newcastle had ended in a near riot in the city streets of Newcastle.

Windows were smashed, petrol bombs were thrown and the now very widely known, thanks to the news, a horse punching incident occurred, in which some crazed Newcastle fan decided to punch a police horse in the face. Shame the horse didn't just bite the bastard's fist off if you ask me!

I wasn't due to work my normal door for this match but as is often the case I got a call and the voice at the other end asked me to work a 1pm till 12.30am shift in a bar on the south of the Tyne, half way between Newcastle and Sunderland, or I would call in it, being from the right side of the Tyne, 'Bandit Country'.

I really didn't fancy it for a start as I like to keep Sundays as chill out days and spend the time with my Son's, but it was Derby day or as I call it 'FUCKING KNOBHEAD DAY!' So I agreed as I know it's almost impossible to get a Doorman on Derby day.

I had never been to this bar before and to be honest hadn't even heard of it but the gaffa had been given my number, but strangely I had a funny feeling that when I got there I would find that I was working a one man door.

So off I went through the Tyne Tunnel into 'Bandit County' and found my way to the bar no problem, a good half an hour early. It was a big bar, and didn't look too bad, one of these chain type bars.

As far as I am concerned, 'One Man Doors' should be illegal full stop, it's just plain wrong. It doesn't matter who you are, how big you are or how hard you are your always just one step away from danger. What is anyone meant to do if there are 10 blokes kicking off at the same time? Or even if there's one, you have nobody to watch your back and it's so easy for someone to just walkup behind you when your ragging someone and stick a glass in your head.

(See the back page and please add your name to the Government Petition to have 'One Man Door's made Illegal.)

The recommendation is to have one Door Supervisor to 100 punters, but that never happens in reality.

So as I locked my car up and started walking towards the bar I saw another doorman standing waiting, a funny looking sort of kid, about 21. But looks can be deceptive as I learned a hell of a long time ago in this game there are two important lessons, never judge a book by its cover, and never ever underestimate anyone. So with the handshakes, introductions and pleasantries complete, we went into a packed bar mainly full of red and white Sunderland shirts, and looked for the manager. She took us around the bar, said what she expected of us, which was all pretty standard, signed in and then we were on the door.

That's when this kid started to annoy me, with his tales of being not so much a doorman, as an all-out warrior on the door. Tale after tale of just how hard he was and what he had done to this one and what he had done to that one. His tall tales got louder and more full of shit over the next half hour and a decent size group of lads standing behind him having a smoke were in fits laughing at him. In the end I couldn't take any more and more or less told him that he was talking crap, talking it far too loud and needed to concentrate on the job in hand.

The bar was in one of those derby days moods, packed full of people from both teams, some ecstatic that Sunderland won, some almost suicidal that Newcastle lost, but all in all not too bad. But there was a certain underlying atmosphere that the place was like a tinderbox, one spark and the whole bar would go up. I was shocked as where the spark that ignited the bar had came from!

So me and Dick, as I am going to call the other doorman from now on, were again at the front door. I was exchanging pleasantries with punters coming in and following the house rule of no football shirts after 5pm, and I happened to turn and see a large man in his forties and two rather large younger girls come out. The bloke had a pint in his hand and straight away Dickie boy clocked it, had I been too hard on him earlier I thought? Then I realized I hadn't as he stood straight in front of the bloke and shouted in his face, "What the fuck are you doing? No drinks outside are you fucking stupid?" Well I don't know who was more shocked at his totally uncalled for outburst, me or the bloke. The bloke with the pint looked at Dick in shock and said "you what mate?" Dick then squared up to him and shouted "Get your fucking pint back in the bar now before I rip your head off".

All of this happened in a flash and straight away my back was up at Dick, what a total dickhead this kid really was!

So that was it. The bloke kicked off, smashed his glass on

the ground and went for Dick who just stood there! I jumped in between them and pushed the bloke back one way and Dick back the other. The bloke began telling me that he had come out to ask for help, and explained that £40 had been stolen from his daughters' handbag inside the bar. I put the bloke in his place a little and told him that Dick had misread the situation and should not have spoken to him like that, but equally I wouldn't tolerate people smashing glasses and going for the doorman.

I told him to wait where he was and told Dick to get inside, behave himself, and find the manager to get the CCTV checked. After what seemed like an eternity, Dick came to the door and told me that the manager was looking at the camera. I told Dick to come back outside on the door and made him and the bloke shake hands. I then took the bloke and his two daughters inside to discuss what had happened and to discuss what had been found on the CCTV with the manager.

It seemed odd at first as something like half an hour later the manageress came down and told him that she was still looking at the CCTV. Anyway the two daughters had a train to catch so I took their details and off they went, leaving me with the Dad.

A barmaid then whispered to me that the manageress wasn't sure what to do, as believe it or not it was the dad caught on camera stealing the money from his daughters' bag while she was at the ladies! Well how scummy can you get? I make no bones of the fact that I hate thieves, but stealing from your own flesh and blood? That is even worse! The bloke was now pretty calm, probably because his daughters had left, so without him knowing, I told the barmaid to get the manager to call the police and that I would keep him talking.

Ten minutes later I saw the police come in behind the bloke, totally unbeknown to him, and go in the back with the manager to check the cameras. Just then I saw Dick letting in a bloke that I had ejected at the start of the shift. I went back towards the door, chucked him out again and had strong words with Dick! I was positioned outside now with Dick between me and the door. I turned round and what did I see? The bloke who had stolen the money holding a chair above his head about to smash it off Dickie boy, and Dick? He just stood there with his mouth open!

I ran towards the chair and pushed it up hard, which sent it flying over the top of the blokes head crashing into a table. I heard a clatter and breaking glass as I grabbed the bloke, who was going nowhere. Filled with rage and fuelled with drink he was as strong as an ox and with no help from Dick I somehow managed to wrestle him into the lobby area and get him in a choke hold with my right arm, holding his left arm with my left arm, his right arm still flying in the air with a naughty looking fist on the end.

So I bet you're wondering what Dick was doing? Well, as shit as he was I expected him at the very least to grab the other arm and give me a hand to restrain the bloke, but no, I couldn't believe my eyes or my ears. He was jumping from foot to foot, throwing air punches shouting and screaming "I'll rip your fucking head off you wanker, I will kill you" I shouted at Dick a couple of times to pack it in and help me, I can't remember what I shouted, but I'm sure I would have shouted something pleasant. "Pack it in you fucking prick before I twat you one!" He ignores this and I managed to throw a kick at Dick catching him in the knee, this brought him back to his senses, 'Phew!' I thought, at last a bit of help here.

Quick as a flash Dick turned on his heels and disappeared. All I could do was hold on to the bloke until the Police, who were in the back of the bar, realized what was going on.

With no radio and stuck where I was by myself there wasn't anything I could do but to hold on, applying just enough pressure in my choke hold not to choke him out, but knowing in myself that if things got any worse, rules or no rules, this thieving bastard was going straight to sleep.

After what seemed like a lifetime, but in reality was just a couple of minutes, the two Police officers arrived. They cuffed his free hand as I removed my choke hold, and with some considerable effort cuffed his second hand and off he went to the van and then the nick.

So, as I mentioned, the atmosphere in the bar was like a tinder box, and thanks to the spark set by Dick the disappearing Doorman and the thieving scumbag; there were now standoffs and shouting matches all over the bar, along with a few glasses being thrown, oh great!!!!!!

So in I went and started trying to calm things down best I could. I began by looking for the main trouble makers and tried my best to get them out of the bar myself. One of the trouble makers did not want to go and as I tried to get him out his friend got me from behind. In a flash I ended up grappling with the two of them on the floor, it felt like I was fighting for my life, outnumbered and by myself. In hindsight it wasn't so bad; the two of them were drunk and half-hearted fighters to say the least. I managed to get up and as I began dragging one of them towards the door, I saw the return of Dick.

So had he had a change of heart? Had he come back to help me? To help me finish what he had started? Did he bollocks. He was standing outside smoking a tab while looking at me through the window. He was watching the goings on with a look on his face like an out of date noodle!

Bit by bit I managed to calm things down. But we were back in a tinderbox situation. Dick was standing on the door and every time I began to walk to the door things started to just about kick off again. 'Enough is enough' I thought, and shouted for the manageress you need to get on the phone and get another Doorman down here, this kid is shite!

She had no idea of what to do and just froze, if I went outside to go on the phone it would have all kicked off again, just then one of the coppers from earlier came back in. I explained my predicament to him and bless this bloke, PC Plod stood in the middle of the bar like a bouncer for me, to keep the idiots calm while I spoke on the phone. I tired everyone I know and they were either working on a door or pissed, there was only one thing for it and that was to ring Dan.

Dan was the doorman that worked with me on the bar where I was head doorman, three nights a week. He also did some shifts in the nightclub that I helped out at. When I first met Dan he was getting the odd shift in the nightclub. On his first ever night on the door, at the tender age of 18, I spoke to him and he seemed a good kid, but over the next few weeks I watched him as he seemed to show a huge amount of potential.

He was great at the 'talking and the walking' as I like to call it, talking someone out instead of dragging or fighting them out. One night I went down to the club after I had finished *my shift and he had a swollen eye, I asked him what had happened and he told me he had broken up a fight and was punched. He told me who the lad was, I had known him for years, fantastic boxer with great promise, but when he hit the drink it all went out of the window.*

Dan told me that this lad had smashed him in the face, "Ouchhhhh, bet that hurt, least that would be you down and out of the game", "No not at all" he said. I was thinking, yeah yeah here we go; maybe this lad was full of shit. "So what happened next then Dan?", "Well he punched me again straight in the face", "So you went down this time?" I asked, "No but it wobbled me a bit!" I was thinking what a shame, at first I thought this lad had the makings of a bloody good doorman, but looks like he is full of shit.

On the way out that night I checked the CCTV only to see that Dan was telling the truth. However he didn't add that after that, he and another doorman managed to get this lad out. So when I found out he was only getting one shift a week, I also found out that the lad that had worked for me at my bar for the last year had had enough and was leaving, and I basically poached him to work for me.

Anyway, I digress. As I said I was on the phone to Dan, my brain kept telling me 'No way you will get him to come out, it's his 19th Birthday' I knew he was my only option. He knew me well enough that I would never ring him on his birthday unless something had gone badly wrong and I had no other option.

So 20 minutes after ringing Dan, he arrived at the bar. I walked over to Dick and said "Right, fuck off home, you have been replaced" I couldn't believe what he said next. He looked at me in the eye and said "Why? Has the manageress complained? I don't think she likes me", the bloody cheek of this jacket filling coward! "Why" I said, "Bloody Why?", "Why do you think, never mind what the manageress has complained about, I am not happy with you. First of all you start trouble in the bar when there was no need, it was caused by you being out of order, then you fuck off god knows where, then you come back and watch through the window, then you don't help me when I actually stopped you from having a chair put through your head! Then, you jump about threatening chair boy!" He looked at me and said "Oh yeah I suppose".

He was still just standing there, the completely useless, spineless, dozy, twonk. I told him to go away and he had the cheek to say, "I will still get paid wont I?" To which I replied "Not if I can help it!"

So with the solid foundation of Dan on the door and me inside we calmed the pub down greatly, and got rid of the remaining few idiots. Surprisingly, we had a relatively peaceful last two hours of the night. With the punters and staff all out, the bar checked and doors locked, the Manageress thanked both me and Dan and gave us a pint on the House.

Much to my surprise she said "Stu, we only have door staff here on derby days, will you do all the derby days for me, but with Dan and not that other Numb Nut?" I told her I was surprised and she replied "You did a great job by yourself until Dan got here, each time you dragged someone out I was so shocked to see you running back in, so just imagine how good it would of been if it was you and Dan all shift; when you didn't have to do everything by yourself".

After a really bad shift and all that had happened, I left the pub smiling. Against all odds, and with the help of Dan, I had pulled it off!

The next morning, Dick must have hunted for me on Facebook and sent me a message saying "By the way, it would seem that my knee is dislocated, it was hurting all day then when that bloke kicked me it hurt more, oh and sorry about needing replaced all night", cheeky little shit even bothering to speak to me! That was him blocked! The funny thing is I told him that it was me that kicked him and not the bloke that tried to hit him with the chair. He thought I was joking, which I found odd because when I had this conversation with him, I was just about breathing fire! I was so angry!

CHAPTER FIVE

The State of the Job

So what happened to this job these days, its nothing like it used to be, it's changed so much, some for the better but fucking hell a hell of a lot for the worse, think back, if your old enough and think about the Bouncers even ten years ago... ... ... But different? Yeah I think so, I think so a lot.

Now the SIA (Security Industry Authority) has a bloody lot to answer for, but believe it or not that's not where the blame lies in my eyes for this 'New Breed' of Bouncer that we have now, over the last say three years it's getting worse, or should I say they're getting worse, now before I go on don't start thinking I am talking about everyone that got the badge over the last few years because quiet simply I am not, I am talking about the ones that are a danger to their team, and to themselves, the ones that shouldn't be on a door, the ones that put others and themselves in Danger, the runners, the cowards, the yellow belly, Jacket Filling bastards that should never ever be on a door.

Now with most of these did they wake up one day and say, "Hmmmm Mam I think I want to be a Bouncer, I think I have the skills and the bottle to be on the Doors", Errrr No I don't think so, they are the ones that are sent on the SIA Door Supervisor Courses by the Job Centre, people that don't want to be Bouncers and shouldn't be Bouncers!

They get pushed into it by the Job Centre, and I have even heard just such a conversation and it made me cringe, a young lad sat there protesting that he was of a nervous disposition and would be afraid to work as a Door Supervisor or even as a Static, or Retail Guard but they kept at him and at him until he agreed, then when they get the badge they are pushed into taking a Door job for more or less minimum wage, and because these people work for minimum wage some companies some venues will just take them on rubbing their hands with glee as they get to maximise profit as the venues will still be charged the same.

So where does this leave the rest of us? The lads and lasses who have been on the Door for years, and the ones coming into it that want to do it and are suited for the job? Well right up shit creek without a paddle if you ask me.

On the one hand the rates of pay don't go up, sometimes I have even heard of rates of pay going down! And it leaves us at risk working with people like the lad above who is of a nervous disposition and will not have our backs. The single most important thing to any Bouncers is to work with a team that they trust, and who they can rely on to have their backs when the shit hits the fan, which it often does!

Quite simply people like this lad are just not up to the job, a lot of them will even admit it themselves, they are bloody terrified! They have never had a fight in their lives and now all of a sudden there standing on a door shaking like a leaf and thinking 'What the actual Fuck am I doing here', and the lads there working with, they can tell. You can tell straight away in many cases, you can smell the fear.

The other fuckers that have also contributed alongside the Job Centre are the likes of G4S in the run to the Olympic Games, they were whacking people through courses and getting them badges like there was no tomorrow, and look how that worked for them? They fucked the whole thing up. But it leaves us with loads of people who shouldn't ever be on a Door with badges.

If you ever watched the Channel 4 documentary 'Bouncers' you will see the perfect example on there, two 'Kids' who got badges this way for the Olympic Games who were 6 stones wet through between then starting their own Door Security business! For fucks sake they had never worked a Door in their entire life and were practicing using a bloody Wendy House in the Garden, and these two knackers seriously thought they could run doors.

So, thanks to the Job Centre's current policy and to the Olympic Games things are now worse in the business than they ever have been before, people don't seem to realise that at times people's lives are literally in their hands, it can be a fucking nasty nasty dangerous job and added to all of this the level of training and preparation in my mind is very far from fit for purpose.

I am really sad to say this but this game in 'Fucked Now', it really is!

CHAPTER SIX

Wheelie Dangerous

Well who would ever think it that people with disabilities would ever pose a threat to Doorman or cause bother, sometimes serious bother? Well why wouldn't they? There normal people just like you and I but people don't seem to realize that, all they see for instance is a wheelchair, or a white stick or someone that has speech difficulties because of profound deafness but no, look past the disability, as with anyone in any walk of life there is good and bad so why should disabled people be any different.

I could tell you all about all kinds of experiences over the years but here's just a few:

I started working in a new bar in a busy resort town and on a Thursday night it was always heaving, absolutely chocka block of students, mucky little devils!

Week after week we would find people bringing in their own drink when we searched them, or when the sly ones got through but there was this one group that we just couldn't seem to catch, one of the group was a lad with no legs, or next to no legs anyway and I thought right then you little bastard I know where the drinks coming in from. I told my other two Doormen my thoughts and had a word with the manager before my little pal wheeled up to the Door and he had a pink fit!

He was of the opinion that because this kid was disabled and in a chair we couldn't search him, well fuck that I thought and to be honest years later I ended up mates with this kid and he really didn't like the idea that he was being treated differently because of his disability either.

Anyway I was so sure that this lad was sneaking booze in for him and his mates that when he rolled up to the door I stopped him and searched him, he wasn't arsed at all about being searched and do you know what I found on him? Absolutely fuck all!

Well the other lads were pissing themselves laughing because I was so sure, and the manager was that pissed off his head was spinning round, and oh how I got the piss taken out of me all weekend and the following week.

So the next Thursday I was ready it was like a personal challenge to me now to find out how they were getting there drink in, so as he rolled up to the door I stopped him again and asked if I could search both him and his chair and he said 'Yeah mate no worries, but what nobody was reckoning on was this, I searched him and his chair and again found nothing, that was until I picked him up, lifted him right out of his chair and found a 2 litre bottle of cider, a bottle of cheap vodka and a water bottle full of Red Wine! I fucking knew it!

Well the manager had almost passed out in shock that I had lifted him out of his chair and the Door Lads were looking shame faced for taking the piss, but the lad in the chair he surprised me and came out with 'Fucking hell mate took you long enough, at least you're the only Bouncer that can see through my chair and my disability and treat me like a normal person!"

In the same bar frequented an old bloke in an electric wheelchair, who stunk of piss, really badly stunk of piss but liked a drink and when I say liked a drink he liked it far too much. I am actually surprised that he didn't get done for drink driving on his way home. Anyway this Saturday night he was shit faced mortal and every time he got pissed he turned into the most cantankerous and perverted bastard you can ever think of.

When he wanted served at the bar he would just drive straight into the people while they were standing there in front of him them waiting to be served, and at a canny old speed as well and the weight of old pissy pants added to the electric wheel chair was quite a bit.

Anyway as I was saying this one Saturday night he was shit faced, he really was and shouldn't have been allowed to get into such a state, I had noticed him giving a couple of the young lasses in the bar seedy eyes, and was keeping my beady eyes on him, just then a new barmaid walked passed, she was tall with a cracking pair of legs on her and a very short skirt.

Here we go I thought, and to my amazement he didn't bat an eyelid as she sauntered past him, must have been the only bloke in bar that didn't mind you, and then he struck. With the speed and agility of a fucking rat up a drainpipe his hand shot up her skirt and a huge grin appeared on his face, and the barmaid jumped about 3 feet in the air and screamed, his other hand shot out at lightning speed and grabbed her leg.

I ran over and said "Come on man, you dirty old bastard you can't be doing that get off her" which he wouldn't so I had to grab his arm by the wrist and squeeze to make him let go of the vice like grip he had on the barmaids leg. "Right mate, you have had enough" I said and he just looked at me.

I tried to push he wheelchair and nothing, then I got my eye on a the controls for the wheel chair where he had the break engaged, I took the break off and used the controls to maneuver him out of the pub, luckily there were a few coppers about so I shouted them over and told them I had just slung this dirty old bastard out but obviously didn't want to just leave him on the street and they said they would make sure he got home ok.

Then we had the big bunch of deaf people that came in a bar I was working at once, now I have nothing against deaf people so before you all start moaning on at me but in my experience it's a fact that deaf people turn nasty with alcohol, even my mate 'Deaf Gary' does and he even agrees! (Deaf Gary was his nickname long before I knew him) so I tell the lad I am working with this and tell him just to keep a general eye out, and sure enough a few hours later they started arguing amongst themselves and pushing and shoving one another, so we got them out sharpish.

Still the kid I am working with wouldn't have it, "Nah man Stu never in a million years, you're taking the piss you", as I laughed and tried to explain that I wasn't taking the piss he just walked off shaking his head.

Well the end of the shift came and the bar I was working on then closed early so it was get locked up and out, jumped in the car and a quick 15 minute drive to a local town to work a nightclub shift, so in we go get signed in and radioed up and as soon as we get inside there are two blokes fighting on the dance floor so we run over and both grab one each, as I get mine in a headlock and start dragging him off the dance floor towards the door to chuck him out of the corner of my eye I see his pal swinging a punch and it caught me right in the left ear. Clump you fucker that hurt!

So I managed to rag this bloke out of the door and I come piling back in and launch myself at the bastard that just twatted me in the ear and start dragging him out, as I do the rest of the group all start kicking off, the lads off the front door start running in and all in all we chuck about 20 out, and can you guess who they were? Yup you guessed it the bunch of deaf people from earlier.

There's still one left in the club shouting going on, no idea of what he was saying mind you and by god this kid was a big lump, like bloody man mountain on stegs! I thought to myself as I was running over 'This one's going to take some getting out', just them I remembered something that my mate 'Deaf Gary' had once told me "Spin them round Stu", he told me "Spin the fuckers round and if they have hearing aid's it fucks them up and they will make a really high pitched squealing that you can't hear, but it fucks up the balance of the mug your spinning round!, Arrrrr what the hell in for a penny in for a pound, so I gave it a go, and do you know what? It worked like a treat!

Apparently the effect of Alcohol on the profoundly deaf are quite well documented and agree with my experience, can't say I have ever checked but that's what I have been told.

Not that much of a story but one bar I worked in years ago we would get a blind bloke in, totally blind with his white stick and he would come in about once a month and he was probably the loveliest bloke you could ever meet, until that was, if he had one too many and it was closing time, when it was time to leave and you would ask people to finish there drinks off you had to give him a wide birth as this bloke could have took on Tyson with that stick, he would just lash out and twat you with it! I was always lucky but I have seen a couple of lads get caught when he swung his stick that was almost cane like and more or less swooshed and cut like a whip!

Last but not least we have the Wheelchair bound drug dealer, this one I suppose shouldn't really be in here but what the hell, it illustrates my point perfectly. I wasn't working as a Doorman but a pub manager at the time, one afternoon I walked back into the bar I was managing at the time, The Musketeer in Forrest Hall just outside of Newcastle upon Tyne, after doing my banking and one of the regulars shouted me over and told me that someone had been selling 'Cowies' in the bar, I asked who and he pointed out a bloke at the other side of the bar, a bloke in a wheelchair.

He must have gone to the Gym because I tell you what the arms on this kid were fucking huge, as I started to walk over to have a word the regular shouted me back and said "Stu, watch yourself he is a nasty bit of work if he gets one of those arms round your neck then you're finished, that's what he normally does". So over I go and say "Mate in want a word with you", then BOOOOOOOOOM out of nowhere he struck out with a his pint glass to my face I tilted my head down and it smashed on my head, luckily for me without really cutting me and him and his mate had it on their toes, well his mate did but he had it on his wheels.

Some months later I left the Musketeer and took the Blue Bell in Shiremoor, and what a bloody lovely place that was, I should have known better than to take a pub that had bars on my bedroom window upstairs.

Anyway when I took the pub on it was fucking minging, a scruffy dirty shit hole, so it was all hands on deck for about three days keeping the bar shut before a grand opening night hoping to get the decent people back in the pub again. Hell I even had a huge bottle of Vodka and a Huge Bottle of Whiskey to give some free shots away. (Courtesy of the Musketeer Stocks ☺)

So I open the doors at 7pm and by 7.30pm we are choka block heaving with people and all was going well, or so I thought until someone came and told me that, in his words, "A Raspberry Ripple is in the bogs trying to knock out pills", right then I wasn't having this so I vaulted the bar much to the amusement and excitement of the punters in the bar, 'Start as I mean to go on I thought' and went piling into the gents and guess who I see?

Oh yes the bastard in the Wheelchair that glassed me in the Musketeer, well I wasn't taking any prisoners this time, I grabbed the handles on his chair swung him round and started getting him out through the bar, all the way he is grabbing for glasses and at one point grabs one from a passing table and again was about to glass me when my mate grabbed it off him, what a nasty scummy piece of work this was.

So I managed to get him outside the bar and next thing he pulls a knife from his pocket, "Don't you ever give up you horrible fucker I said", and then I don't know what came over me but it was the only cause of action that I could think off, I wheeled him into the middle of the road, which was a bus route and kicked in the spokes of his chair in so that he couldn't move and left him there, going back into the pub.

I checked back ten minutes later as hadn't heard a collision and he was gone, god knows how but he was gone.

Not something that I am proud of but it had to be done.

I never saw him again for the best part of 20 years when he started wheeling himself into my bar in Whitley Bay, where he was promptly told to fuck off, he gave me a load of verbal not recognizing me, until I said "Look mate, fuck off now or I will take you into the middle of the road and help you wait for the next bus!" With that he trundled away!

The moral of the story is 'Never ever under estimate ANYONE' able bodied or disabled. Don't discriminate against the disabled, for good things and bad!

There's no difference you get good and bad, sad and mad in every walk of life so why should someone with a disability be any different?

CHAPTER SEVEN

The Breadstick

A long while back now, standing on the door on a damp, wet, winter night thinking to myself is this actually worth it anymore? Standing in the rain sick as fuck, quiet night and no action what so ever and the bar staff were bloody slow with the coffee's this week as well. Little did I know that my night was about to be livened up no-end!

It was the second night I was working with a new lad, big lump his was, and if I am honest I reckon he was a 'Steg Head', all juiced up! You know the kind all steroids and bad attitude. Anyway the big lump was milling about and I was imagining my nice warm bed.

Say what you want but I swear 99% of decent doorman would say that these kind of nights are the worst, these are the kind of nights that drag, standing for hours on end, basically with fuck all to do, hardly any punters and working with a lad that has absolutly zero banter! No crack, no nothing. I can't stand nights like this. I really can't. You stand there thinking of your family at home in the warm, longing to be with them. Almost frightened to look at your watch as time passes at half the speed of usual, or at least it seems that way. All the time still knowing that you have to stay alert and switched on as you never know, you just never ever know when it might kick off.

Doesn't matter if you have ten punters in your venue, one hundred, or one thousand, the potential is always there. If your off the ball, not ready, half asleep or whatever, potentially you're going to get hurt, or in my eyes just as bad your mate that you're working with can get hurt if you are half asleep and don't have his back.

Anyway, here I am waffling on and you're all thinking, 'OK Stu, but what the actual fuck has this got to do with a Breadstick. Well up to the door walks this big 'Fugly' Bastard, all snide 'Lacoste' tracksuit and no teeth! Well that's a lie, he did have a few teeth, and in fact teeth like a council fence!

You know the kind, they think they have all the gear but really they have no idea!

Apart from the obvious fact that I could just sense that he was dickhead before I he was close enough to tell that he was completely and utterly of his Tits, blatant to see, chewing his lips off, white shite round his lips and pupils so big a dilated you could have parked a bastard Landover in them!

(Remember Fugly from the first book? Fugly = Fucking Ugly!)

So he walks over to the door, with a strut like he really is 'somebody', and I think to myself, 'Not a hope in hell pal, he looks at me and to be fair he knew what was coming, "Not tonight mate, your not coming in here in that state", he just stood for a second or two staring at me, with me staring back. I knew what he was doing and it wasn't going to wash with me, I have had many other 'stare downs' over the years and many of them with much bigger and better than this clown.

As soon as he realized that I wasn't going to drop my arse he started trying to give it the big lad, "What the fuck you going to do to stop me coming in like? Do you know just who the fuck I am?", deep down I was pissing myself laughing at this overgrown monkey, if I had a quid for every time someone had said this to me then... ... ...

"Mate if you don't know who you are then how the fuck am I supposed to know who you are? Tell you what don't ruin your whole night and just walk away from my door, try your luck somewhere else as there is no way in the world you're coming in here". Just then two of his mates came rolling up behind him, you have seen the movie 'Reservoir Dogs', well these two were strutting up the street like 'Reservoir Puppies'!

So now joined by his two mates he thinks he is invincible now, proper 'Gangsta' this kid, my arse is he, fucking plastic gangster at best! "I am coming in you prick" he shouts at me, now I know it's going to kick off, so changing my stance quickly I see just how this is going to play out, at the same time wondering if the big 'Steg Head' who was working with me had my back. I had the feeling that he didn't but if I had turned round to check this would have been a sign a weakness and I wasn't going to show him that. "I am taking over this bar, I have a shotgun in my coat and I will blast the fuck out of you!" he screamed.

Well this was going to be fun I remember thinking as he suddenly lurched forward towards me, as he did I jumped and grabbed him in a headlock and brought him down to my size, but I was surprised just how strong that he was as I tried to drag him away from the door, as the struggle turned into a fight I felt this was one that I wasn't going to come out best, still with him in a headlock he is kicking and punching, still with him in a headlock I gave him a couple of digs to the face but they weren't doing much so I decided that I had to put him to sleep.

I tightened my grip around his neck and was planning on choking him out, looked like I was on my own as 'Steg Head" wasn't helping me out, what choice did I have? Maybe he was having bother with his two little mates, the Reservoir Puppies?

It's amazing what goes through your mind in situations like this, sometimes I think it's because you get so used to doing this job your mind wanders and you think of all kinds of mad stuff. In fact a mate of mine told me that he once has some trouble with four blokes and was taking a bit of a beating and all he could think of that was he was hungry and what he was going to have for his supper when he got home. This you might think is a bit far-fetched but if you knew my mate Colin then you would understand!

As my grip tightened I tried to shift my weight behind him to have more leverage for the choke but as I did this the ferocity of this tosser got worse and somehow we ended up crashing through the doors of the pub and over a table and chairs, like a real wild west bar-room brawl, glasses smashing and people screaming we still fighting rolled over the table and land hard, very hard onto the floor with me smashing my back and shoulders on the way down, him on top of me trying to punch still and me trying my best to stop him, then it happened, probably the worst mistake he made that night. The absolute horrible piece of shit started to sink his council fence teeth into my cheek, at first it felt like a nip and them started burning as the pain of him breaking the skin began.

Well that was it, in that split second all I could think of was my kids and how they would feel if I had a lump bitten out of my face, nah I wasn't having this and it was then I lost my temper and I mean lost it big time, I managed to lift one of my legs and booted him for all I was worth in the chest, he fell backwards and off me with the this kick and it really had fucked him for a few seconds, straight away like a fucking rat up a drain pipe I am on him raining punches down on his face and head, blood now pumping from his mouth and nose then he bellows "That's it that's it I am done, I am done", I stop at this point really wanting to kick this cunt in the ribs, hard and fast hoping to feel his ribs crack and splinter under my boots but somehow I managed to control myself and he got up and ran followed by his two mates into a taxi that was hanging about outside, as I am getting my breath and feeling for how deep that damage is on my cheek the taxi pulls away and then spins round at the opposite side of the road and stops. The big wankers face a bloody mess he hangs out of the window shouting "I will get you, I will find out where you live" and other assorted bullshit comments and then off the taxi went.

I look down and see a soggy mess of broken glass, spilt beer and blood, and right in the middle a little souvenir, one of his teeth!

So, you're still wondering about the breadstick?

Well, a few weeks later I had just finished work at my day job, all suited and booted I go shopping on the way home at my local Tesco's and as I wander round who do I see but this toothless, scroate. He is staring at me and I look him up and down like a piece of shit and carry on with my shopping. He just disappears but I keep my eyes in the back of my head just in case but he is nowhere to be seen as I head up towards the bakery and grab a French stick before heading to the tills to pay for my stuff.

As I walk out of the shop with a carrier bag in one hand and a French stick in the other there the mug is standing staring and he rips he t-shirt off and starts shouting "Come on then you bastard", why the hell people pull their shirts off like this I will never know, just makes them look like a total knobhead if you ask me!

Well he got a fright at what happened next, I had to do something as he was in-between me and my car so as he is jumping about like a kangaroo on a fucking pogo stick *playing the big man I drop my bag of shopping and go at him, not thinking I swung my weapon of choice, well not really of choice but without thinking I smashed him in the face with a French stick as if it was a baseball bat, well it couldn't have hurt, it was a bloody breadstick, unless he got crumbs in his eyes but he let out a yelp like a wounded cat and turned and ran up the car park with me in hot pursuit with my breadstick, as he got to the fence I thought that I had him cornered, in fact so did he for a second I think as he stumbled and fell I reigned down blows on his face and head with the breadstick and he is howling now like a cat with a rocket up its arse and he managed to climb through a hole in the broken fence and off he ran!*

I started laughing, real laugh out loud laughing, that was until I looked down and saw the state of my French stick!

CHAPTER EIGHT

'Tony the Stamp'

So there I am nice early finish in the bar I am working at and I decide to have a quick pint after work so I walk up to a local Nightclub that I work on sometimes and when I get to the door theirs a big fella absolutely completely fucking rat arsed pissed, arguing the point with one of the blokes of the door, my mate Tony.

The bloke is holding out his hand and showing him a stamp on his hand, it's the stamp from the club, he had obviously been in earlier when he was monged off his Tits and got a stamp. As I stood watching Tony got this slight grin on his face and said to the bloke "Right mate, two seconds just wait there" and off he went, the other two lads at the door making sure this big drunken lummox didn't get in.

After a good five minutes Tony came back, now we had no idea what he was up to but normally if Tony takes the piss, it's bloody funny and worth waiting for. "Mate let's see that stamp on your hand again" so the drunk bloke holds his hand out to show the stamp, Tony then pulls a thick black marker out of his pocket and draws a cross on top of the stamp, carefully puts the lid back on the pen and puts it in his pocket, then turns round to the bloke and says "Look mate, its invalid your stamp, have a look yourself see there's a cross over it, invalid".

The bloke looked at his hand for what seemed like an eternity, with all us, including Tony going bright red trying not to laugh and the bloke shook his head and said "Arrrrrrrrrrrrrrrrrrrrrr yeah, invalid" and turned around and walked away off up the street with a soundtrack of a load of Bouncers pissing themselves laughing!

CHAPTER NINE

The Boot Ride

Well Saturday night and I am on my way to work, me and Tommy who I have worked with for about a year on the same door, and just when I am looking for a parking space my phone starts ringing, I didn't recognize the strange mobile number that was flashing on the screen as the phone warbled away like some kind of incessant wailing of a pissed off baby. I pull in outside of the Kebab shop to take the call and I hear a woman's voice that I didn't recognize, a Scottish woman's voice, "Who's that" I say into the phone, "Och its Marie" said this harsh Scottish voice. "Marie" I said still non the wiser who are you, "Och you know it's me Marie, Steve's Girlfriend". Steve was a mate of mine who used to drink in my bar sometimes with his girlfriend, always very paranoid and a funny type of a kid, a Chef by trade that seemed to drift from job to job to job endlessly and always wore the same jacket.

Wondering how she got my number, and at the same time thinking that it must have been from Steve I say "Right ok, I am rushing to work pet, what do you want", she hums and har's for a bit and then says "Well Stu, you know how I am away home to Scotland to see my family for the weekend", "Yeah Steve mentioned you were off Haggis bashing for a couple of days, why?", and then the whole thing comes out, something that left me in an awkward situation and something I really didn't want to know about.

So as it all unfolds she tells me that she is not actually in Scotland with her family, but getting ready for a night out just a mile or so up the road at a local hotel with people from the office and lab where she worked, which incidentally I always had the feeling was the kind of place that got cute little bunny rabbits and put shampoo and tabs in their eyes for research or something nasty like that.

"Right then, number one Marie why are you telling me this and number two why have you told Steve that you're in 'Sweaty Sock' country".

Then she spat it out, and I really really didn't want to hear this, with her voice sounding sort of nervous she says, well there's sort of a night out from work and we will be in your bar later, please don't tell Steve that you have seen me". By now I am seriously in danger of being late for work so I just said "Yeah yeah whatever it's got nothing to do with me" and I put the phone down. As I quickly parked the car up me and Tommy walked to the bar to start our shift and the dodgy phone call from Steve's bird was lost from my mind.

So we get in the bar, sign in get radioed up and do the normal checks and it was a particularly busy night, from walking into the bar until walking out that night we had a steady stream of pissed up knobheads to fuck off out the bar, quite a few of them getting ragged out by whatever means necessary, so when Marie walked up to the bar a little sheepishly with her work mates I couldn't really be arsed with whatever skulduggery she was up to, silly bitch I thought playing games. So in she came with a load of her workmates and again said, "Stu, please don't tell Steve that I am here and not in Scotland", to which I replied a little annoyed now, "I don't give a fuck where you are or what you're up to just don't

Fucking involve me ok?", and in she went a bit red faced.

Now this is where it started getting interesting and alarm bells started ringing, in my day job by coincidence in the office that I worked in from at the time happened to be office 'Frankenstein's Lab and Office' and often on the way in or out of work I bumped into a bloke that was a delivery driver of some sort from 'Frankenstein's Lab' where the 'Sweaty Sock' worked, as I had worked there for years and years and so had he we sort of knew each other enough to say hello, but it's not something that I have really thought about and had never put two and two together that he must have worked with the 'Sweaty Sock'.

So when he came wandering up the street very sheepishly by himself I said "Alright mate, the rest of your lot are in there", "Who, who's in there he said" like I had just poked him in the eye with a burnt stick, "The people from your work mate", I replied just at the same time that the penny was starting to drop, "Oh and Marie" I said. When I said her name he went bright red and just hurried into the pub, I knew what was going on here, the driver and the 'Sweaty Sock' were obviously having a game of hide the sausage without Steve, Marie's boyfriend knowing and without the drivers wife knowing.

'Oh for fucks sake' I thought, 'why me, why do I have to be told about it', and before I could ponder on it any further I heard the breaking of glass and shouting and screaming just inside the bar and had to run inside along with Tommy, my trusty sidekick to break up a fight, between two men who were regulars and normally the best of mates. Both in their mid 50's you would think they would be old enough to know better! By the jist of it while dragging them out like two

Pregnant hippos, one fat bloke had been slipping the other fat blokes daughter one and he was not amused. It was all happening tonight. Dirty beggars!!

So the night went on and me and Tommy were rushed off our feet, it was one of those nights where it's just one knobhead after another, after another. When I was doing inside checks I could see the 'Sweaty Sock' and driver getting drunker and drunker and closer and closer, "What a complete Piss take" I muttered at them at one point when I passed, with about an hour left to go until closing time the rest of 'Frankenstein's Lab sauntered out, good spirited and slightly worse for the wear but not too bad, leaving the gruesome twosome behind I remember noticing.

About 20 minutes s later someone came to the door and complained that there was a man in the ladies toilets, so up I go like a startled gazelle and with all the grace of the Ark Royal, I bang on the ladies door and shout "MALE STAFF!" and in I go, the smell hitting me straight away like a brick smashing me in the face, the pungent aroma of cheap perfume, alcohol and piss, mmmmm lovely, NOT!

Surprise, surprise, surprise guess who was just about to get pulled into a toilet cubicle? Yup that's right you guessed it 'Delivery Boy', I promptly grabbed him by the arm and with no airs and graces slung him out of the ladies, his face as red as an over ripened tomato, and come to think about it he had a funny shaped head like a squashed tomato as well, now why didn't I notice that before then? Anyway he is stuttering "I I I I Am sorry Stttu, Sorry don't tell annnnyone please", pathetic little shit! When I told him to get out before I gave him a slap he was out of the door like Lindford Christie on Whizz! Boooom He was out of there!

And then out comes a very embarrassed Marie, before she can say anything I interject with a friendly little phrase kept for just such an occasion, "You dirty fucking bitch, I tell you what go on fuck off out of my bar before you spread the clap all over the place, you're a complete an utter rotten skank, you fuck off!", well I thought that I was rather benevolent putting it that way, and I have no idea why she seemed to have taken offence. Her face was just like her thighs! (Like Thunder)

But this didn't last more than about a second or so and she got a big cheeky grin on her face, grabbed me cock and tried to pull me into the toilet with her! Well that was enough, I have never been an angel with women or anything else and I don't claim to be but she was purely and simply extracting the urine, this was my mate's bird, the bird he was head over heels in love with and who he even shared a flat with. "Right Slut, OUT! NOW!" I told her struggling not to bellow so loud that Sam Cleveland would have heard. (My mate from Australia) and out she trudged.

So I get back to the door being expertly looked after by my mate Tommy and when I tell him he thinks it's hilarious, "Steve's a big wet dozy sad cunt, you should have done her mate" he said, "Nope not my style that" I replied, still feeling pretty disgusted.

So it soon came to the end of the night, the amazing sound of the bell being rang that told everyone it was time at the bar, and no more drinks. We give it five minutes and then start and 'coax' everyone to see there drinks off and leave, as the minutes roll on we have an almost empty bar with the exception of one punter, as always, the most ignorant white haired, scruffy, sad, insignificant pile of wart juice that I have has the displeasure to meet in my life, who was always the last one there. Standing talking shit as normal. Anyway as per we have to tell him to go, and with a check of the toilets and whatnot we get locked up, sit down get our feet up and have a nice chilled out relaxed pint.

As me and Tommy are sitting we are discussing what I should do about Steve, and his trollop of a bird. Tommy just sat laughing, finding it hilarious, to be fair I did a bit as well. But what should I do, keep my gob shut and not mention the fact that his beloved 'Sweaty Sock' wasn't up in Scotland with her mother having Haggis sandwiches for tea and was in fact no doubt at this very moment getting rattled all over the Hotel by the Delivery Boy!!

Every time I thought about it like that I kept bursting out laughing and every time I laughed Tommy laughed, and when Tommy laughed I laughed more, I suppose you get the drift? So I decide like all good leaders, to put the decision off until tomorrow, like a greasy Spanish waiter saying 'Manjana, Manjana' I was basically dropping out of making the choice of what to do. So we finish our pints, no more than one mind if I am driving and out the backdoor we go saying bye the Manager, still laughing as we are walking round the corner past the top of a back lane I see Steve's car, that's odd I thought he should still be at work frying chips and peeling spuds or whatever the hell he does at work, the lights of his car were on but were very dim, as I get closer I see Steve sitting in the dark in the car without the engine running with his head slumped on the steering wheel.

Straight away Tommy says, "look the sad fuckers topped himself because his tart is getting strumped off the delivery boy", looking at him and realizing the battery was flat on his car it did cross my mind as well! "Steve, Steve mate you ok?" Just then I saw movement and he lifted his head and with a face like a smacked arse and tears running down his cheeks he said "Where is she Stu? Somebody seen them in the bars round here, I have been driving round and looking all over for them and been sitting here for over an hour waiting to see is they walked past'.

"I can see that mate, you should have turned your lights off first" but he wasn't arsed about his car just Marie McSporan and the Delivery boy, so at this point I really didn't have any choice in the matter and told him everything. Didn't like doing it but better hearing it from a mate I suppose.
He just looked at me blankly and said "help me start the car I want to go home"' so turning round to see Tommy wandering across the road towards it with a large 'Elephants Leg' (Donna Kebab) I shouted "Tommy man you greedy bastard come and give me a hand to push Steve's car will you?, so hungry Horace saunters over wrapping the now half of an elephants leg up and putting it in his pocket and we push the car for Steve to bump start, which took a while the stupid cunt didn't know you needed to put it in gear, never mind that was him sorted, hungry Horace still had half of an elephants leg and I just had a very bad feeling as I watched Steve drive off like a bat out of hell.

"Come on Tommy mate, I have a feeling that I know where he is going!", so we walked the rest of the way down the street to get my car, and drove up to the Hotel where the 'Sweaty Sock' was supposed to be saying and whose car was in the car park? Yup Stevie boy. He was ringing and ringing and ringing the reception desk from the car park, who were putting down the phone on him after he had been kicked out of the hotel because they wouldn't tell him what room she was staying in.

He just wouldn't leave it, and kept going back to the door and kicking off with the security, well a really old fella who was really just a night porter but give the bloke his due he was doing a bloody good job. I went over and ragged him away this time and said sorry to the night porter, he said "It's not your fault mate, but if this Bell End doesn't fuck off I am going to have the call the law and get him nicked".

Just then an idea popped into my head, not sure where it came from but it worked anyway. I started walking towards my car, I had a big Chrysler 300c at the time which was just perfect for what I had planned, "Steve come with me mate I said, I have got just the very thing in the boot", "Eh, what do you mean, what you got" Steve spat, "Mate just the very thing to get her out, come and look at this" just as I said that I popped the huge boot lid with me keys and said "Get a look in there, that's what we need" and as he looked down into the boot I lifted up his legs and flipped him straight into the boot and shut the lid.

Well Tommy was fucking pissing himself laughing, he thought this was great and then turned round and said "What we doing now then? Tell you what Stu I am not digging a fucking hole for a shallow grave", crackers this kid. Anyway we jumped into the car and drove out of the hotel car park with him in the boot banging and shouting, well that was soon remedied as I blasted the music so we couldn't hear him. As we were pulling out of the car park a police car was pulling in, 'Fuck I hope they don't know I have him the boot, I don't want to get done for kidnapping', anyway it drove straight past and obviously they were looking for Steve so looks like I was just in the nick of time.

We pulled up outside of Steve's house and Tommy was still pissing himself laughing, he was having a great night, so by now my reckoning is Steve is really mad and as soon as I open the boot he is going to come out fighting, I didn't want to have to twat my mate one, he was having a bad enough time to start with, so staying in the car, I popped the boot and true to form he jumped out and was off!

Well that was my good deed done for the night, I knew that the Scottish Tart would leave the hotel as soon as she seen the coast was clear, well I thought so anyway so by the time Steve ran all the way back to the hotel (Bless Him) she would be gone, and maybe then he would behave.

As I found out next day he ran all the way back and she was gone, but get this what do you think the cheeky cow did? She only waited in a taxi until she saw him coming back to the hotel and then went home. So with a heavy heart when Steve got home he was shocked to find her waiting in bed supposedly asleep and denying the lot, saying that she had got half way to Scotland and changed her mind and came home while he was at work.

The fucking cheeky bitch, can you believe that. Steve by all accounts seemed to just wipe what happened out of his mind, simply pretended that it never happened, and after all this he married her and went to live in Scotland!

I still think one day she will wind up dead at the bottom of a Loch somewhere!

CHAPTER TEN

Thuglife

When will I ever learn, that's what I always say! Time after time at a busy Nightclub by the Sea that I have worked at on an off for years I manage to get stitched up by my good mate Tony, the Head Doorman!

I have worked with Tony on and off for years both at a Nightclub and doing some special jobs like minding 'JLS' and Glasgow Band 'Glasvegas' doing book signings and personal appearances, top bloke great Doorman and funny as fuck in a dry kind of way.

Anyway he has this thing where if someone's been chucked out and there giving it the mouth and want back in and ask for the manager, he will say, "I'm not the boss, Stu's the boss" and point at me! Doesn't matter if I am working or not, he still does it and I still fall for it.

So this night two Nigerian lads are in the club, ones not to bad and the other thinks he is a cross between 'King Dick' and fucking 'Mike Tyson', you know the kind real plastic gangster. So he is strutting round the club by all accounts grabbing women and shoving blokes out of the way, well he made the mistake of feeling up the wrong lass, in more ways than one as she turned round and punched him in the face.

Shocked as I reckon he thought he was onto a winner with old the skank, that combined with the fact that he thought he was king of the fucking world he started kicking off and trying to get hold of her to punch her back.

This was just before I got there and by all accounts the lads who work inside had dragged him out, and he started kicking off outside threatening all kinds, just as I walk to the front door! I wasn't working there that night I had been working another door and it had been a long hard night, I had just finished and was going to the club for a well-deserved bottle after work, tired and grouchy as I walk to the door I see the massive black bloke kicking off, so on go the gloves.

I may not have been working there that night, but that makes no difference at all as far as I am concerned, we are all in the same job 'No matter who's tie you wear' in my eyes and if the lads needed a hand out when I was there bang up for it.

Then the immortal words, "Nah mate I am not the boss, him there, Stu, that's the boss", so round he came squaring up to me and ranting and raving, out of the corner of my eye I saw one of my mates videoing it on his phone, 'Cheeky little fucker!"

So, he is out of the bar so I decide to humour him, talk to him and get rid of him that way, but as always is the case with drunken knobends he went on and on and on, so in the end I started getting annoyed and said "Look mate, you boring me now, I have been good enough to talk to you but now you're really boring me so FUCK OFF!"

Now what he did next I think was supposed to intimidate me, but it worked the exact opposite and I just started pissing myself with laughter! He shouted at the top of his voice "WARRIOR, I AM A WARRIOR, THUG LIFE FOREVER", while punching the air and jumping up and down. Warrior ha, my fucking arse you are pal. Dickhead yes, Warrior errrr no!

Between my raucous laughter I say "Look Warrior, go fuck off before I give you a slap, go on off you fuck!" He looked at me like he was going to cry and shouted "THUG LIFE, I AM THUG LIFE!" and then lifted up his shirt to show a huge tattoo on his stomach that said "THUG LIFFE", well this made me laugh even more. And no that's not a typo Life had actually been tattooed onto him with the incorrect spelling of 'LIFFE'.

As much as I found it funny, he was starting to annoy me now, so I give him a shove, a good hard push with my palms open to his chest sending him flying, across the path and into the road, and by the time he knows what is happening I am on him again in his face and shout "Right Warrior Fuck Off now. Before I really get pissed off" and off he went walking across the road.

Now the best bit of the lot is what happened next, he is standing with his mate straight across the road staring at me, just as some random bloke walked down the street towards him, well he was random to him but not to me, he was one of my mates and just as he walked past him boom, right hook straight to the chin!

Thug life warrior knobhead is out cold before he hit the ground, well we all just fell about laughing then, as quickly as my mate knocked him out he was gone. I didn't ask him to do it, I didn't even know he was out but the lad, and ex unlicensed boxer later told me, "Well it serves the cunt right".

Well he hit the floor 'like a bag of boiled shite' and it took a good few minutes for him to come round.

Thug Life, More like Mug Life I thought to myself.

CHAPTER ELEVEN

The Ferry

Going back a hell of a lot of years now, up popped up one of those 'One Off' Jobs, is was on a Ship of all things. Now you think a lot about the floating luxury hotels that pass for ships these days, and how lucky I was getting some graft on one of these, but you would be wrong. Very very wrong.

I was told that the job was on a cruise but this was no cruise liner, this was a vessel named the Shieldsman, a ferry that normally crosses carrying passengers from North Shields to South Shields, but tonight it was out on a 'VIP River Cruise'.

VIP? VIP? VIP my fucking arse was it, of course unless VIP stood for 'Very Idiotic Pissheads' that is! But the money was good and could it really be that bad on a corporate party on the Ferry? 'Nah should be fine I thought', so I agreed to do it.

The Ferry as setting off from South Shields at 7.30pm on the Saturday Night and coming straight to North Shields when it set off and was due abut 7.50pm to pick up some party goers from the North Side, so I was going to join at North Shields

along with another bloke, I didn't know who. If I had done I don't know if I would have done that job!

So I get ready and drive down to North Shields Ferry Landing, parking my car in the Port Hole Pub carpark asking my mate who has the pub to keep an eye on it for me and walk to the ferry landing, and who is the first person I see? Well if you read my first book you will know this man well, Charlie who I worked with at 'The Working Mens Club' and true to form guess what he had in his hands? Only a bloody flask of Tea and a HUGE packet of his favourite Custard Creams, as I walked towards him I just thought 'Oh Fuck, it's going to be another one of those night's'.

"Hello Stu mate, I heard you were working on here as well tonight, we will have a right old laugh" said Charlie. "Yeah I am sure that we will mate, me doing all the graft and you drinking you tea and stuffing you piggy face with biscuits all night I bet".

He didn't look to happy with what I had said but you know what, after the last time I worked with this 'Walter Mitty' I didn't really care. In my eyes the only way to work in this game is as a team, nobody, doesn't matter who you are can handle everything by yourself, you need to work together and have each other's backs and most of all, probably the single

most important thing in this game, especially when the shit hits the fan is trust. Sometimes that's all you have, that's all that you rely on when the shit really hits the fan and you go in.

I don't care what anyone says, everyone feels fear at times, especially in this game, anyone that doesn't at times feel fear is either a liar or not right in the head! But fear is good, it can give you the edge if you can overcome that fear and what you need to overcome it is trust in whoever you're working with, the kind of trust that you now whatever happens, no matter how bad it gets then the person that you're working with will not hide, not turn and run but will stand side to side with you and fight to the death if need be. That fear, if you channel it right can be turned to adrenaline and that is what gets you going.

Anyway, I didn't trust in Charlie, not after the last time at the club, but I had said I would do the shift and when I say I will do it then I will do it. I am not one of these that drops people in the shit at the last minute, never have been, never will be.

So as we are waiting for the Ferry to pull in a few party goers are milling round also waiting to get on-board and Charlie is chatting shit at me same as always, talking some load of old fanny about how this reminded him of when he was in charge of training the 'Navy Seals' of all things but I learned a good lesson some time ago with this joker, basically that he was totally and utterly and completely Full of Shit!.

So I just more or less ignored him and chatted with some of the people waiting to Party, as we watched the ferry leave South Shields and sail over to North Shields. As it was about half way across the Tyne you could hear the music blasting out. I can't remember now what the song was but it was the middle of the summer and it was the big summer hit of the time that everyone liked, it grew louder and louder and it came closer and closer and finally docked at North Shields.

So I make sure the people who were joining the party all get on safe and get on-board and go see the gaffa of the job, Phil and get bit of brief. We hang on five minutes in case anyone was a bit late and get a couple of stragglers on and set off, we are underway and start to sail off from the Ferry landing

when I notice I can't see Charlie. "Phil mate, have you seen Charlie?" I ask, "No mate, I thought he was with you" he says. Well I thought he was with Phil, I look back to the ferry landing and would you credit it, there he was the dumb fuck, drinking tea from his flask and dunking his custard creams like he didn't have a care in the world.

"Phil", I shouted "look back to the Ferry Landing mate", well Phil's face was a picture when he saw him. "The stupid twat " Phil shouted as he ran up to the wheel house to ask the skipper to turn back to pick him up. To be honest as he used to train Navy Seals, my arse did he, I am surprised he didn't just swim to the ferry.

As we turned back I rang him and it took him an age to answer while he finished slurping his cuppa and put the lid back onto his flask, "Charlie for fucks sake what are you doing, why didn't you get on" I said, "Oh err I didn't notice you all leaving". Well for god's sake how can you not realise that we were leaving I remember thinking to myself, so we docked back at North Shields again and on he gets.

Phil wasn't happy with him, he wasn't happy at all, this was his first job to run on the booze cruise up the Tyne and he had put in for the contract, so all eyes were on us tonight and this wasn't a good start.

So once again we set off, the music is blasting and the drink is flowing and we are just really standing around as so far everyone is well behaved, but the nature of the game I knew that this wouldn't last. So first of all we sail East as if we are going to leave the Tyne and go out of the piers to sea, as we got near to 'The Bar' as it's called locally, the sort of line

between the two piers that you can always feel when you leave the Tyne and go out to see, as the boat sort of lurches down and back up in less than a second and we turned around and headed slowly back past

North Shields Fish Quay, past the old ship yards which at the time were a sad reminder of what ship building on the Tyne used to be like, like graveyards to heavy industry. Before the regeneration.

The further up the river we go the more pissed people seem to get but for the first few hours it was all good humoured. Then I heard bit of a ruckus towards the small gents toilet, I ran to take a luck and here I found two blokes pushing and shoving each other, I jumped in the middle and said "Come on lads for fucks sake, what's the crack", it took a good while to get it out of them but finally I found out what was going on, it turned out that one of the blokes was a dealer and had short changed the other bloke who was trying to but some sniff (Cocaine)from the dealer and he had actually sold him whizz (Speed) instead.

I searched the bloke and found a lot of gear on him, all in tiny bags ready to sell. But in the middle of a river what the fuck was I supposed to do? So I took all of the gear from him and made him watch as I chucked it straight into the Tyne.

For the amount of gear that was there the fish would have been off their Tits for weeks. The Dealer was gutted and was giving me daggers, I managed to get a message to Phil who spoke to the skipper and we pulled into a small old slip way dock somewhere around Wallsend, and basically chucked him off the boat, it was a bit like making him walk the plank. I also wanted to chuck the other bloke who had been trying to buy the gear off but Phil wouldn't let me, it turned out that the bloke was the CEO of the company who had hired the ferry. Talk about setting a good example for your staff!!

So with that sorted, on we went with the trip, we had to tell a couple of pissheads to stop climbing on the rail, for obvious reasons as I didn't have any intentions of jumping in after one of them, Charlie was with me and then he just disappeared.

Par for the course with this dickhead, but after an hour when I still couldn't see him I got a bit worried. Phil who was sitting with the Skipper in the Wheel House hadn't seen him either.

Eventually I found him, and from what I saw I wished that I hadn't, I found him in the ladies toilet giving it to a huge fat

Woman in her mid-fifties, as I opened the door all I could see was his arse going up and down between two huge fat legs with his pants around his ankles.

"Charlie man for fucks sake, what you doing shagging 'Munters' when I am left to do all the work myself, as soon as he heard me he jumped up off the 'Swamp Donkey' and pulled his pants up, "Sorry mate" he said but with this idiot sorry just didn't wash.

When he stood up from between the huge fat legs it was a terrible sight, I think it's possibly scared me for life. This big big old 'Swamp Donkey' was stuck, no pants on and no knickers, her legs were so fat that she ended up wedged with a leg down each side if the toilet and jammed between the toilet and the wall, legs 'akimbo'.

I am sure that you can just imagine the sight, and that I don't need to elaborate any further, but I tell you what, I have never eaten a Kebab since, but the sight wasn't the worst, the smell was overpowering. Dirty scruffy bitch, so I ended up getting one arm and Charlie the other and we tried our very hardest to pull her up but she just wouldn't budge. I went to shout for Phil to get a hand, and I did warn him about the abuse that his eyes and sense of smell were about to get but he didn't believe me.

He walked back in before me to find a red faced Charlie, standing there can you believe dunking custard creams into his tea again! "Charlie man, you dirty scruffy bastard, how the fuck can you stick it in that "shouted Phil, and by the look on his face and the way that he screwed his nose up I wasn't the only person to be scared for life that night. So this time with the three of us we tried again, but we just couldn't get her up, each time we tried she screamed, her legs were firmly jammed between the toilet pan and the wall.

As me and Phil were talking about what we were going to, that cheeky bastard carried on munching on his custard creams, crumbs shooting from his mouth as he chewed, eventually I came up with an idea! There were caterers on the Ferry who were feeding the crowd so I ran up the stairs, steep as they were taking them two at a time just waiting for the fresh air to hit my nose and my lungs and to get rid of the repugnant stench that seemed to be everywhere. It was like 'The Fish Quay Gut' on a hot day.

I went to see the gaffa of the catering firm and explained the predicament that we had, and with a laugh he gave me a catering pack of margarine, the plan was to grease 'Big Bird' up and get her free. As I thanked the catering guy he shouted me back "Stu, from what you have said I don't fucking want the marge back mate"!

So as I got back down there and explained my idea Phil said "Right sounds like a plan, go on then grease her up Stu", "Fuck off Phil there is no way in the world I am going near that thing, Charlie Boy was fucking her so he can do it"!

What amazed me was Charlie at first refused to touch her, 'so it was ok to play hide the sausage with her but not to touch her, funny kid this, but anyway one look at Phil's face and knowing his liking of severe violence when the mood took him seemed to be enough and off to work he went, greasing her up.

Then she started kicking off "Fucks sake hurry up, this is my husband's work party he will be wondering where I am. 'Poor fucker' I thought not only was she cheating on him getting it in toilets but she is an ugly stinking Munter as well. But saying that I had half a feeling he might be pleased with Carlie, maybe if Charlie was fucking her then he wouldn't have to.

And then what happened next, I wouldn't have believed in a thousand years if I wasn't there to see it actually happen, she was all greased up me and Charlie got a leg each and Phil grabbed her hands, we pulled and pulled and she still wasn't budging, we pulled again and this time she started to move and I went flying backwards crashing into the door and ending up flat on my back still with her leg in my hand, but she was still wedged I took one look and nearly shit myself and let out an involuntary scream thinking for a second that I had pulled her leg off and threw it away from me, hitting Phil in the head with what turned out to be a false leg!

I seriously wasn't expecting that, and there she was still wedged there, 'Legs aKimbo' or should I say 'Leg aKimbo'. Whatever we did we just couldn't get her out so there was only one thing for it, we had to get the Ferry diverted back to South Shields Ferry landing and call the Fire Brigade.

That left Charlie a huge problem, there was now no way that her husband wouldn't find out that he was slipping her one on the toilets, Phil was fuming and I don't blame him, there wasn't much chance of him getting the contract now. This was a total disaster. As we were pulling into the ferry landing totally unbelievably Charlie pulled out his Custard Creams again and offered them around, he must have felt guilty as he didn't normal share them around!

When he offered Phil one with a stupid grin on his face I think that must have been the final straw, "You have got to be fucking joking Charlie, you really must be taking the

absolute fucking Piss" and then out of nowhere Phil launched one of his legendry punches, a straight right to Charlie's chin.

The Custard Creams flew up in the air and Charlie was out cold. "Stu, sort that cunt out will you" he says, well I thought this was hilarious at last he had got what was coming to him and he hadn't even seen the husband yet. He came round a few seconds later and said "Fuck that felt like a freight train smashing me in the face, it's a good job I like him or I would put him to sleep for a long time, I used to be in the SAS you know, I know the techniques, I could kill him with my bare hands". "That's right Charlie, I will go tell him will I" I said, "Errr nah Stu don't please mate don't". Booooom the sound of Charlies arse dropping.

As the fire brigade boarded the boat and made their way down to 'Old Hot Lips' to get her free me and Charlie made our way back on deck, he was just trying to make a sharp exit off the Ferry and onto South Shields Ferry landing when a bloke came flying up to him shouting and swearing and pushed him square in the chest, so hard that he flew back over the rail and straight into the river!

As I watch him splashing around, shouting and waving his arms, I just say to Phil "Hot Lip's Husband I presume"!

CHAPTER TWELVE

The Robbery

It had been a mad bank holiday weekend, I had been working the full weekend in a faceless Yorkshire town, the same as the next town and the next and more than likely the next one to that, but in this town at least it was different, they had a tradition going back 100's of years, in fact so many bloody years that nobody even knew why the fuck that they did it. Handed down from Father to Son, Mother to Daughter a tradition of running or walking the very perimeter of the town, or the 'Walking of the Boundaries as they called it, the Women must go Clockwise and the Men anticlockwise, this was meant to ward off evil spirits but looking at some of the women in this 'Arse Hole of Nowhere' it didn't work. I think to be honest it was just an excuse to be on the piss all weekend.

Anyway as all of the locals, without fail were involved, I shipped me and my lads down to cover, a good earner for the Lads and an even better one for me. We had done it the year before and knew what to expect, not difficult work, but long hours, very long hours. The one saving grace was I suppose the bar that we worked was huge with a hotel attached so we just kipped down there as the travel would have been a Killer. We were working from 11am Saturday morning for a straight 12 hours, the same on the Sunday and then on the Monday 10am until 1am the following morning when we would travel home and I was back in the office for my day job at 8am on the Tuesday morning so it was going to me a massively tiring weekend but bloody good money and going by last year it was a good laugh, especially with the lads of the normal door team who were on the piss for the three days and nights.

So we pull up outside the bar in the middle of a market type town centre square that was pretty much all but closed off to traffic now and filled with fairground rides, hotdog stalls and all of that kind of thing, it was 10am Saturday morning giving us just enough time to chuck the bags in our rooms and straight on the job, the couple that managed the bar were pleased to see us as we had good banter with them the year before and they knew that we were a good tight team that were professional and good at what they did, but also liked to have a laugh.

There were the four of us, 3 I would say good lads and one 'full of shit' but I had to take who I could get again this year being a bank holiday weekend. There was me, and two old mates of mine Kev and Ronnie, we were the three good lads and then the 'Full of Shit' lad, Charlie who I had worked with a couple of times both ending in disaster as all he seemed to give a shit about was cups of Tea and Custard Creams!

So anyway we dump our bags in the rooms and head down for some food before we start, the manageress of the pub shouted for us and said she would do some food for us, which meant it was free and free food, along with anything else is always the best. So not long after four huge English Breakfast's were on the table in front of us, but there was only three of us, yep you guessed it Charlie had gone walk about already, he said he was going for a piss and never came back, I swore to myself then that I would never use him again for one of my jobs, never mind work with him again.

We had all finished and were sitting drinking Tea at 10.45am and in comes 'Brain of Britain', Charlie with two shopping bags filled to bursting, "Charlie man for fucks sake, will you stop wandering off all the time, it was bad enough on the

Ferry so don't start your shit again". With a look of a scolded child this 6ft odd Monster looked at me and said, "Well somebody had to go get the biscuits, didn't they lads?" I should have known he had been off to the local supermarket and bought about 3 tons of 'Custard Bastard Creams'! I could see straight away that I had made a mistake with him, in fact to be honest he was a last resort, 'Lazy Bastard'!

So he wolf's down his breakfast like the pig that he was, and off we go to our positions, what we did last year worked well so in decided that we would do the same thing again, we had one man inside, two on the door and one outside managing the crowd in the large beer garden, already I wanted to take of Charlie's Head so I decided to put him inside for the first rotation.

So as I crack open the front door I am more or less blinded by the sunshine, at least it was going to be a nice day, better than last year when it was pissing it down all weekend, outside is a massive queue of people already, at least 300 strong and all gagging for the first pint, 'God this place must take a fortune over this weekend' I remember thinking to myself.

A quick radio check and all good apart from Charlie, and after shouting a couple of times I get a reply that confirms just what I thought, the bastard is munching his Custard Creams already! So as I start letting them in the bar soon fills up with half of them in running gear ready for the madness of 1pm where they run or in some cases walk the boundaries of the town, not sure how that works mind for the ones that take it seriously and seem to have all the gear and no idea after two hours in the boozer, but there you go!

So in they come, some cracking on that remember us from last year and I am keeping an eye out for a bird that I want to avoid from last year too, all sober and good natured as is normally the case before they start drinking, before you know it the pub is full, completely rammed to capacity and you just can't get moved inside or outside in the beer garden. This as I have said wasn't a bad job just long hours, oh and the fact that most of the buggers wanted to bring their own drink in with them, and they must think we were fucking stupid because you could see them going into the supermarket across the road, come out with bottles of vodka or cans and then when they try and get into the bar they aren't carrying it anymore but have a budge in their coats, but as much as this was a pain in the arse it was also a nice perk of the job as we confiscated it all and of course kept it!

So 12.45pm comes round and the bar empties quicker than it filled, all of them ready to go 'Walk About', but of course they all wanted to take their drinks with them, so after last year we had it sorted with a lass from behind the bar brining out a couple of big bottle bins, one for the plastic glasses and one for the bottles, I had Charlie for once in his life actually doing something and stopping them at the door with drinks and getting them chucked in the bins, or with these lot most of them knecked the drinks first!

So a few hours with a handful of people left in the bar meant a nice chill out time before the madness began once again, with ice cold soft drinks on tap we relaxed in the blazing sun of the beer garden until they all started heading back.

When they did a lot of them looked half dead, and off to the business of the day to get slaughtered.

All in all it was a good weekend, with very little trouble. A couple of minor fights and one of them was funny as fuck, a bloke in his eighties tried to start a fight with a lad about twenty, for no reason at all so as we got him out he stands there staring at me outside, his face dead pan and comes out with "Come on then lad, you're not from these parts, me and you right now a straightener in the field behind the pub", I couldn't quite believe what I was hearing, all eyes were on me when he says "Right then, old school son take your shoes off, me and you in the field" and he sits down on the ground and starts to take off his socks and shoes, the first shoe came off followed by the sock which took some doing as this bloke was absolutely shite face drunk, then he was half way through taking off the second shoe and get this, he nodded off to sleep the poor old fucker.

Sound asleep snoring and slavering just in time for his two sons to come walking up the street, apologies to me and carry him home. This according to them was a common occurrence!

Apart from that the weekend went off more of less without incident, just a few chuck outs for people being mortal, before we know it its closing time Bank Holiday Monday, we get all the punters out and as we are going to sit at the bar and have a drink, and get squared up for cash I ask that lads what they all want to drink, when Charlie comes out with another bizarre slightly messed up thing, "No nowt for me Stu mate, I am going for a shite, can't wait it's my tradition that you never shite on a Bank Holiday weekend so I been holding this in for days, and the tortoises head is well and truly out of its shell", I looked at Charlie totally bemused and the other lads did too, anyone else I would have laughed thinking that it was joke but not him!

"Right then Charlie but don't be long I want to hit the road soon ok, oh and go and check that all the doors are locked on your way to the Shithouse", I say and off he goes.

Five minutes later I hear the back door bang but think nothing of it thinking its Charlie, more fool me as the next thing I know some bloke all ski-masked up is standing there holding a sawn off shotgun, we were only getting fucking robbed! The first thing I thought was that I was an idiot telling Charlie to check the doors!

As we are all standing there with this idiot shouting "Give me all the fucking money" the manageress has tears pouring down her face, and to be honest I wasn't too happy myself, then in the distance I hear the toilet flush, but the masked raider didn't seem to here.

I was looking at the other two lads from my squad and they were looking at me, all of us looking for the slightest flicker in each other's face's, if one was going to go for the cunt with the gun then we all were, but as it turned out we didn't have to.

Round the corner came Charlie, cup of tea in one hand a packet of, yup you guessed it Custard Creams in the other and just as he rounded the corner the masked gunman turned to look at Charlie just as Charlie looked at him. Charlie let out a scream, a high pitched scream that I can only describe as that of a 9 year old girl if someone shoved a firework up her Barbie Dolls arse and lit it!

"Stu man, you bastard you know I don't like masks" he shouted, thinking that it was me with the mask on messing about and then he swilled, the masked raider still thinking it was me in the face with a scalding hot cup of tea! The shotgun clattered to the floor but luckily didn't go off and the three of us all jumped on the robber with the burning face while Charlie stood shaking not knowing who the fuck was who as he saw me, then I think realizing that it was a real robbery.

So, Charlie a hero? Really? Well that's how he was billed in the local paper down there and he has dined out on that story for years, obviously adding his own twist to it about how he used his special forces training and what not, he even has the newspaper cutting on his wallet!

But... ... ...We know the true story... .....Don't we?

CHAPTER THIRTEEN

Snow Way!

Getting ready for work in the middle a December a couple of years back, an 11pm until 3.30am shift in a local nightclub, I had worked there on and off over the years and got on really well with all the lads on the Door, Bar Staff and management, it had been snowing that day and snow was still thick on the ground, a complete white out as I set off for work.

As I pull into the car park of the hotel that the nightclub was part of the snow was still thick on the ground which is unusual being so close to the sea, I get out of the car with another lad who was working there that night and then I hear it "Help, Help, Help", looking around I couldn't see anyone and thought I must have maybe imagined it.

Then again, "Please Help me, please Help", I still couldn't see anyone so started looking up at the hotel windows thinking maybe someone in the hotel was in trouble and needing help. Over the years there has been some funny goings on in this hotel so you just don't know. In fact just a few weeks before someone had tried to top themselves.

I had been on the front door and a taxi driver I knew came running over and said "Stu, Stu quick round the front there is a van just revving and revving", well in didn't think much of this at first but he was insistent so I went to look and what I found was alarming to say the least.

I big white van, I think it may have been a Renault Traffic but couldn't be sure was revving as hard as it would go constantly, there was fluid of some kind pouring from the engine, I later found out that the radiator was burst so it must have been water and antifreeze.

All I could see in the cab was smoke, literally full of exhaust fumes so as I ran down the steps to the hotel car park I had a bad feeling, when I got to the driver's window there was a bloke in the driver's seat sitting completely slumped over the steering wheel, I tried the door and to my relief it fell open, the exhaust fumes hit me as soon as the door opened burning my eyes and my lungs with each breath that took, I grabbed the keys from the ignition killing the noise of the engine, I then made a grab for the bloke and started to drag in him out.

The thing was he didn't want to get out, eventually I managed to wrestle him to the ground just as the manager of the Hotel and Nightclub came running round, followed by the Police. There were empty cans of Carlsberg Special Brew all over the cab of the van and he was shitfaced as well as half dead from the Carbon Monoxide Fumes, the Police saw to him and took him to hospital, and as I looked in the van I saw a modified tube coming into the cab from the exhaust.

I later found out that it was a deliberate attempt to kill himself after a domestic on the phone with his Mrs. and he had done the same thing many times before. Bet the company he worked for were sick as fuck as he kept wrecking their vans!

So as I am looking up to the Hotel windows, I could still here a voice shouting "Help, Help me please", then what I can only describe as a 'Blitzkrieg' of snowballs descended down on me and my mate.

Looking all over we couldn't see where the hell they were coming from, or the person that was shouting help, then just a brief glimpse of a baldy head across the road hiding behind the wall that led to the beach, so quick as flash I popped the boot and grabbed out the spade that I had in the boot, always handy for the snow and even more handy if you need to bury a body in a hurry, and ran across the road to twat whoever this was with the spade, then all I could here was laughing, both behind the wall and behind me now where the voice had been coming from that was shouting help.

Then I saw them, just in the nick of time, Neil my mate and one of the Doorman and Jonny the Manager, Jonny with a radio in his hand shouting "Help, Help" and laughing.

Absolute bastards, they had it all set up, lying in wait for me getting to work, they had hidden another radio under a car and were using that to pretend they were shouting for help, knowing full well that I would try and find out who needed help, which would distract me nicely while they pelted me with snowballs!

They got me good style, my revenge the next night was piling loads of snow up under Neil's wheels so he couldn't pull away and Jonny, always the joker built a 3ft high snow Cock on the roof!

CHAPTER FOURTEEN

One Man Doors

I have worked many so called 'One Man Doors' over the years and no matter how good or bad you are, no matter what the venue is like, no matter what the clientele or like I have come to the same conclusion as any other right minded person would come to and that is 'One Man Doors' need to be made illegal.

I have been lucky over my career as a Doorman and especially lucky when I have, against my better judgment worked a 'One man Door' until I decided finally enough is enough. I have been threatened with a needle after starting a shift and ejecting a Junkie, had a knife pulled on me when getting in between two men fighting, need I say more?
The use of one Door Supervisor working alone needs to be outlawed and made illegal as this puts lives at risk. Unless legislation stops this practice then Venue's will continue to risk the lives of Door Supervisors in order to save money. Please take a moment to sign this government ePetition to outlaw this dangerous practice!

http://epetitions.direct.gov.uk/petitions/63180

For further reading on this issue please take a look at the 'National Doorwatch' website www.nationaldoorwatch.org

CHAPTER FIFTEEN

So, you want to be a Bouncer?

If you want to join the ranks please Visit
www.safersecurity.com

Owner and senior trainer at Safer Security, Paul Rooks has been working in the private security sector for over 30 years. Paul the senior trainer at Safer Security, has written many of his own courses covering such areas as Self Defence for Doorstaff and unarmed combat for bodyguards along with handcuffing for security operatives.

Paul is a fully qualified, very experienced and fully insured Un-armed Combat Instructor, Close Protection Instructor and Teacher Trainer. Paul has worked for many years within the UK as a Door Supervisor and Bodyguard and has also had extensive experience in Eastern Africa in such countries as Kenya, Uganda and Tanzania, since 1994.

Paul also works as a Security Consultant assisting people managing their events and running their training contracts. Paul has an extensive history working in frontline Door Supervision and as a Bodyguard, this was many years before the SIA licence system came in to operation but he also has embraced all SIA training and activities and studied to gain all of the modern qualifications needed to run an approved awarding body centre and to instruct to the SIA and Award body standards.

So you want to be a Bouncer? Then do it.........
With Safer Security www.safersecurity.com

Knives not Lives

After meeting Steve Cairney and becoming friends at some BBAD Bare Knuckle Boxing events and hearing the tragic story of Leon his son, I am a huge supporter of his campaign for awareness.

Being a father to three sons brought this home all the more to me, and also working as a doorman I have faced issues in regard to knife crime on a number of occasions. When I was made aware of Steve's campaign I knew that I had to try and help. If by having Leon's story in all of my books just one life saved then it is more than worth it. Knife crime is all to prevalent in this day and age and people don't stand up and be counted, Steve is standing up to be counted, and both now and in the future I will be there to support Steve in his courageous campaign.

Choose Live, Not Knives!

Stu Armstrong

Choose Live, Not Knives!

My Son, Leon came out of school at the age of 15 and enrolled with the army at the age of 16, determined to make difference in the World. He did tours in both Afghanistan, Bosnia, Ireland and was a keen boxer who represented the army and got in to the finals in Germany. He came out of the army when he was twenty, due to losing one of his army pals in a road side bomb.

Once he came out the army he started to work with his dad, within demolition and progressed well within this new career path. He had just started a young family and had two little girls (The girls now are at the age of five and three). Leon had worked with dad for the past five years and was a very happy, positive young man and a lot going for him.

On the 22nd December 2012 when Leon was at twenty five years old, my wife and I were called at around 2.30am by a person at the door who mentioned that he thought that Leon had been stabbed. I got dressed and told my wife that everything would be OK and ran down the street and into a back garden, where someone was trying to resuscitate Leon.

I pushed him out of the way and fell to my knees and picked my son up in my arms and eyes where as bright as stars and body as cold as ice and told him he would be OK, because his dad was here. The knife was still stuck in Leon. The next thing, the emergency services where there but Leo was pronounced dead at the scene.

A few days later we had to identify the body and we had to wait two months to bury him. The whole family was torn apart. It has only been the last few months until we have been able to restart building our lives.

We would not want any family to go through this. **NO PARENT SHOULD EVER HAVE TO BURY THERE OWN CHILD.**

CHOOSE LIFE NOT KNIVES.

A big thank you to Stu Armstrong for all his support and raising awareness to others via our sad loss and story, If we could stop one family going through this heart ache, nightmare and grief, then the above made a difference.

Rest in peace oor son Leon Cairney!!!

For more information please visit www.livesnotknives.co.uk

Stephen Cairney

ABOUT THE AUTHOR

Stu Armstrong is from North Shields in the North East of England and is first of all is a loving a proud father of his three amazing sons, by day he is Implementation Consultant, by night he is a Doorman with 19 years of experience. From a very early age Stu has loved books and been fascinated by words and the power of the written word, an ambition has always been to write a book.

Stu's first book, The Diaries of a Doorman, was written & self-published in December 2013, with a zero budget and he was lucky enough to have some very good friends who helped him with artwork, proofreading and Stu's oldest son helped with the photography.

'The Diaries of a Doorman - A collection of true short stories' was a smash hit success from first launch achieving fantastic 5 star Amazon reviews, and prompting a fan base who have been asking for Stu to write a follow-up book!

Since the original publication Stu Armstrong has announced

that by sheer public demand and the amazing sales and reviews of his first book 'The Diaries of a Doorman – A Collection of True Short Stories' that a follow up 'The Diaries of a Doorman Volume 2 – Bouncers & Bravado' will be out in spring 2014. Stu is now working on a Novel which is still un-named but is sure to be a smash hit and will take readers through a story that follows one man through a decade of his life and will have readers on the edge of their seats and will take them through every emotion.

For more information about the Author Stu Armstrong please visit www.stuarmstrong.com

Facebook.com/stuarmstrongauthor
Facebook.com/bookdoorman
Facebook.com/bookdoorman2

@stuarmbooks

Made in the USA
Charleston, SC
17 June 2015